A CUNEIFORM ANTHOLOGY
OF RELIGIOUS TEXTS
FROM UGARIT

SEMITIC STUDY SERIES

NEW SERIES EDITED BY

J. HOFTIJZER AND J. H. HOSPERS

N° VI

A CUNEIFORM ANTHOLOGY OF RELIGIOUS TEXTS FROM UGARIT

AUTOGRAPHED TEXTS AND GLOSSARIES BY

JOHANNES C. DE MOOR

AND

KLAAS SPRONK

LEIDEN • NEW YORK • KØBENHAVN • KÖLN

1987

Library of Congress Cataloging-in-Publication Data

A Cuneiform anthology of religious texts from Ugarit.

(Semitic study series, ISSN 0169-9911; new ser.,
no. 6)
Texts in cuneiform script.
Includes glossaries.
1. Ugaritic language—Texts. 2. Ugarit (Ancient
city)—Religion. I. Moor, Johannes Cornelis de,
1935- . II. Spronk, Klaas. III. Series.
PJ4150.Z77C86 1987 492'.6 87-23821
ISBN 90-04-08331-6 (pbk.)

ISSN 0169-9911
ISBN 90 04 08331 6

PRINTED IN THE NETHERLANDS BY E. J. BRILL

CONTENTS

PREFACE

The present collection of religious texts from the kingdom of Ugarit is intended for use in classrooms. It is *not* a critical scientific edition but an eclectic and idealized text which should confront the student with as little epigraphic problems as possible while at the same time enabling him or her to acquire the necessary familiarity with the Ugaritic cuneiform script. Unfortunately it has become a tradition in the teaching of Ugaritic to work from transliterated texts. The current handbooks contain only some very limited cuneiform samples at best. As a result one often comes across proposed restorations of damaged passages that are physically simply out of the question. Scholars are not accustomed to copying out their ideas in cuneiform.

The Ugaritic alphabetic script is not difficult to master. We think students should be trained from the very beginning to read it in its original form. Students should also be encouraged to add alternative readings of their own or proposed by their teachers. Any sign standing between square brackets has been restored by the editors of the present manual and should in principle be regarded as doubtful.

Dotted signs are damaged on the original tablet, < > indicates supplemented signs, { } superfluous signs, ! marks an emended sign.

No introduction or commentary is furnished. The teacher is supposed to supply these or the student must consult other literature for this purpose. A simple alphabetical glossary was added, however, as was a list ordering the lemmata according to semantic categories. The latter may be useful if the student is looking for suitable terms to restore a broken passage. We thank Miss Marjo Korpel for her assistance in preparing the glossaries.

Kampen, 1986

KTU 1.101:1-10

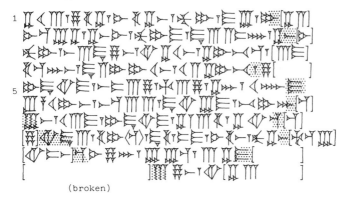

(broken)

KTU 1.3

I.1*

20 [cuneiform text]

25 [cuneiform text]

(broken)

II.1 [cuneiform text]

5 [cuneiform text]

10 [cuneiform text]

15 [cuneiform text]

20 [cuneiform text]

25 𒑱 ...

30 ...

35 ...

40 ...

III.1 ...

(broken)

3ᵃ [...]
3ᵇ [...]
3ᶜ [...]
3ᵈ [...]
3ᵉ [...]

5 ...

10 ...

15

20

25

30

35

40

45

IV.1

5

10

15

20

25

30

35

40

45

47a

47b

50

55

V.1

5

10

15

20

25

30

35

40

(broken)

VI.1

5

10

15

20

25

(broken)

KTU 1.1

II.1

5

10

15

20

25

(broken)

III.1

5

10

15

20

25

30

(broken)

IV.1

5

10

15

20

25

30

(broken)

V.1

5

10

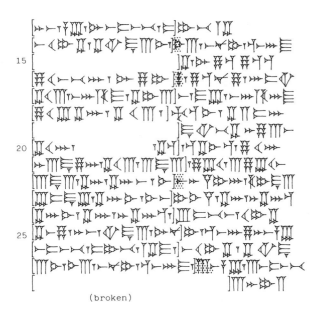

(broken)

KTU 1.2

35 [cuneiform text]
   [cuneiform text]
   [cuneiform text]
   [cuneiform text]
   [cuneiform text]
40 [cuneiform text]
   [cuneiform text]
   [cuneiform text]
   [cuneiform text]
   [cuneiform text]
45 [cuneiform text]
   [cuneiform text]
   [cuneiform text]

                    (broken)

II.1 [cuneiform text]
     [cuneiform text]
     [cuneiform text]
     [cuneiform text]
  5 [cuneiform text]
     [cuneiform text]
     [cuneiform text]
     [cuneiform text]
     [cuneiform text]
 10 [cuneiform text]
     [cuneiform text]
     [cuneiform text]
     [cuneiform text]
     [cuneiform text]
 15 [cuneiform text]
     [cuneiform text]

                    (broken)

III.1 [cuneiform text]   [cuneiform text]
      [[cuneiform text]
      [[cuneiform text]

(broken)

1

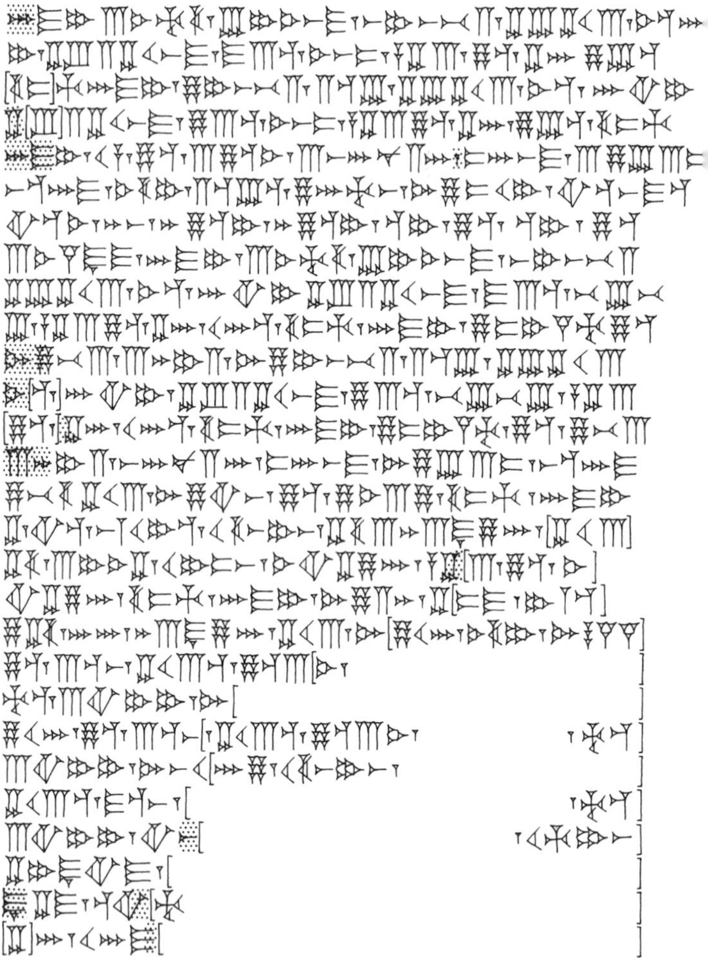

(broken)

KTU 1.4

I.1 [

⸢𒀭⸣

]

[⸢𒀀⸣ ⸢𒀀𒀀⸣ 𒀀𒀀𒀀 𒀭 𒀭𒀭𒀭 𒀭𒀭𒀭 ⸢𒀭⸣ 𒀭𒀀 𒀀 𒀀𒀀]

5 [𒀀 𒀭𒀭𒀭 𒀀𒀀 𒀭𒀭 𒀀 𒀭 𒀀𒀭𒀭𒀭𒀭𒀭 𒀀𒀀]

[𒀭𒀭𒀭 𒀀𒀀 𒀀𒀀 𒀀𒀀𒀀 𒀭𒀭𒀭 𒀭 𒀭𒀭𒀭𒀭 𒀭𒀀 𒀀]

[𒀀𒀀𒀀 𒀀𒀀𒀀 𒀭𒀭 𒀀𒀀 𒀀 𒀭 𒀭 𒀭𒀭𒀭 𒀀𒀀 𒀀𒀀]

[𒀀𒀀 𒀭𒀭𒀭 𒀀𒀀𒀀 𒀀𒀀 𒀀 𒀭 𒀀𒀀 𒀭]𒀭

[𒀀𒀀 𒀀𒀀𒀀 𒀀 𒀀𒀀 𒀭 𒀀 𒀭 𒀭𒀭𒀭𒀭 𒀭 𒀭𒀭𒀭]

10 [𒀀 𒀭𒀭𒀀 𒀭𒀭𒀭 𒀭𒀭 𒀀𒀀 𒀭 𒀭 𒀭𒀭 𒀀𒀀]

[𒀀 𒀭𒀭 𒀀𒀀 𒀭 𒀀 𒀭𒀭 𒀭 𒀭]

𒀭𒀭𒀭𒀭𒀭 𒀀 𒀭𒀭𒀭 𒀭 𒀭 𒀀 𒀭𒀭𒀭𒀭

𒀭𒀭 𒀀𒀀 𒀀 𒀭 𒀭𒀭 𒀭𒀭𒀭 𒀭 𒀀𒀀 𒀭𒀭 𒀀

𒀀𒀀 𒀭𒀀 𒀀𒀀 𒀭 𒀭𒀭 𒀭 𒀭𒀭𒀭 𒀭

15 𒀀 𒀭𒀭𒀭 𒀀 𒀭 𒀀𒀀 𒀭𒀀

𒀭 𒀭𒀭 𒀭 𒀀 𒀭𒀭𒀭 𒀀𒀀 𒀭 𒀭𒀭⟨𒀀⟩ 𒀀𒀀 𒀀𒀀

𒀭𒀀 𒀭𒀭𒀭𒀭 𒀭 𒀭𒀭𒀭 𒀭𒀭 𒀭 𒀀 𒀀𒀀 𒀭𒀭

𒀭 𒀭𒀭 𒀭 𒀀𒀀 𒀀𒀀 𒀭𒀭 𒀭𒀭 𒀀 𒀭 ⟨ 𒀭𒀭𒀭 𒀀𒀀

𒀀𒀀 𒀭 𒀭 𒀭𒀭 𒀀𒀀 𒀭 𒀀𒀀 𒀭 𒀭 𒀭

20 𒀀𒀀 𒀀𒀀 𒀭 𒀭 𒀀𒀭 ⟨𒀭⟩ 𒀭 𒀭 𒀀𒀀 𒀭 ⟨

𒀭 𒀭 𒀀𒀀 𒀀𒀀 𒀭𒀭 𒀭 𒀀𒀀 𒀭 𒀀𒀀 𒀭 𒀭 𒀭

𒀭 𒀭𒀭 𒀭 𒀭 𒀀𒀀 𒀭 𒀭 𒀭 𒀀 𒀭 𒀭𒀭 𒀭

𒀭 𒀭 𒀀𒀀 𒀭 ⟨ 𒀭𒀭𒀭 𒀭 𒀭 𒀭𒀭𒀭 𒀭 𒀭 𒀭 𒀭

𒀭𒀭 𒀭𒀭 𒀭 𒀭 𒀭 𒀭 𒀭 𒀭 𒀭𒀭𒀭 𒀭 𒀭

25 𒀭𒀭 𒀭 𒀭 𒀀 𒀭 𒀭 𒀀 𒀭 𒀭 𒀀𒀭 𒀭𒀭𒀭

𒀭 𒀭 𒀭 𒀀𒀀 𒀭 𒀭 𒀭𒀭 𒀭 𒀭 𒀭 𒀀 𒀭 𒀀𒀭

𒀭𒀭𒀭 𒀀𒀀 𒀭𒀭𒀭 𒀭 𒀭 𒀭 𒀀𒀀 𒀭 𒀭 𒀭𒀭 𒀭

𒀭 𒀭 𒀭𒀭𒀭 𒀀𒀀 𒀭 𒀭 𒀭 𒀭

𒀭𒀭 𒀭 𒀭 𒀭 𒀭𒀭 𒀭 𒀭 𒀀𒀀 𒀭 𒀭 𒀭 𒀭

30 𒀀 𒀭 𒀭 𒀭 𒀭𒀭𒀭 𒀭 𒀭𒀭𒀭 𒀭 𒀭 𒀭 𒀭𒀭 𒀭 𒀭

𒀀 𒀭 𒀭 𒀭 𒀭𒀭𒀭 𒀭 𒀀𒀀 𒀭𒀭 𒀭 𒀭𒀭𒀭 𒀀𒀀 𒀭 𒀭

𒀭 𒀭 𒀀𒀀 𒀭 𒀭 𒀭𒀭 𒀭𒀭𒀭 𒀭 𒀭 𒀀𒀀 𒀭𒀭

𒀀𒀀 𒀭 𒀭 𒀭 𒀭𒀭 𒀭𒀭𒀭 𒀭 𒀀𒀀 𒀭 𒀭

𒀭𒀭 𒀀𒀀 𒀀𒀀 𒀭 𒀭 𒀭𒀭𒀭 𒀭 𒀭 𒀭 𒀭𒀭 (𒀭𒀭𒀭!)

35

40

(broken)

II.1

5

10

15

20

25

30

35

40

45

(broken)

III.1

5

10

15

20

25

30

35

40

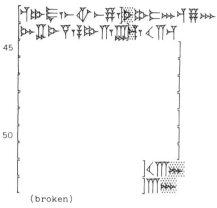

45

50

]⟨𝕀𝕀𝕀⟩
]𝕀𝕀𝕀

(broken)

IV.1

5

10

15

20

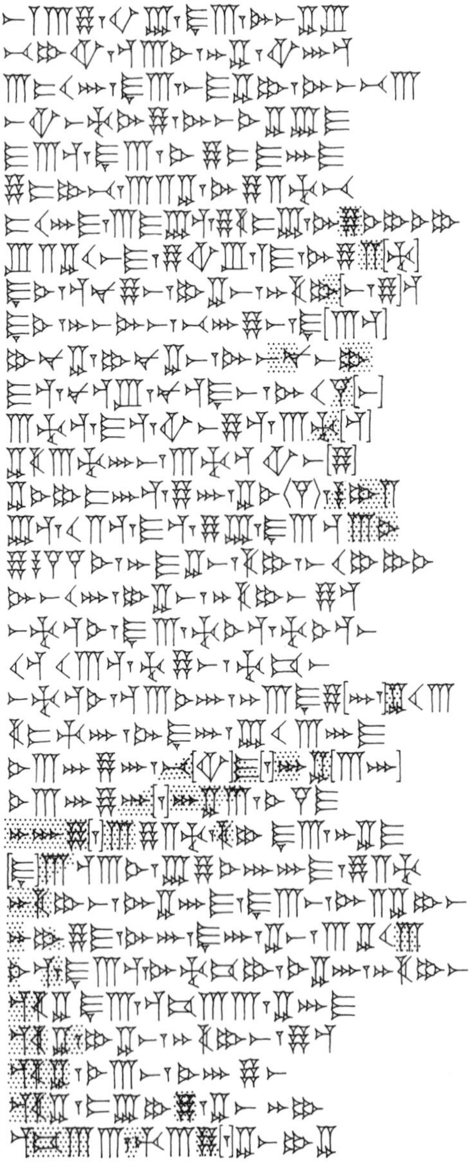

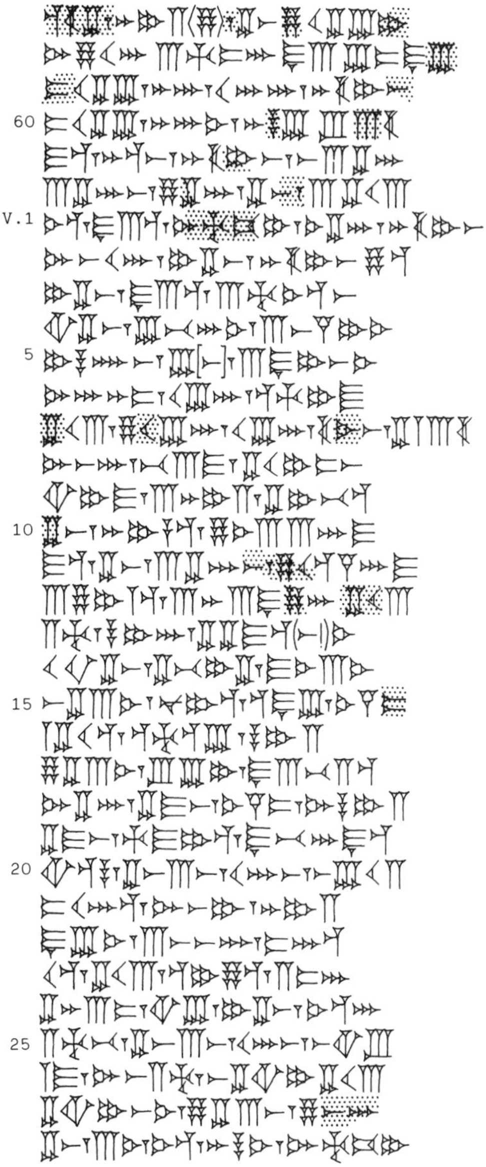

30

35

40

45

50

55

60

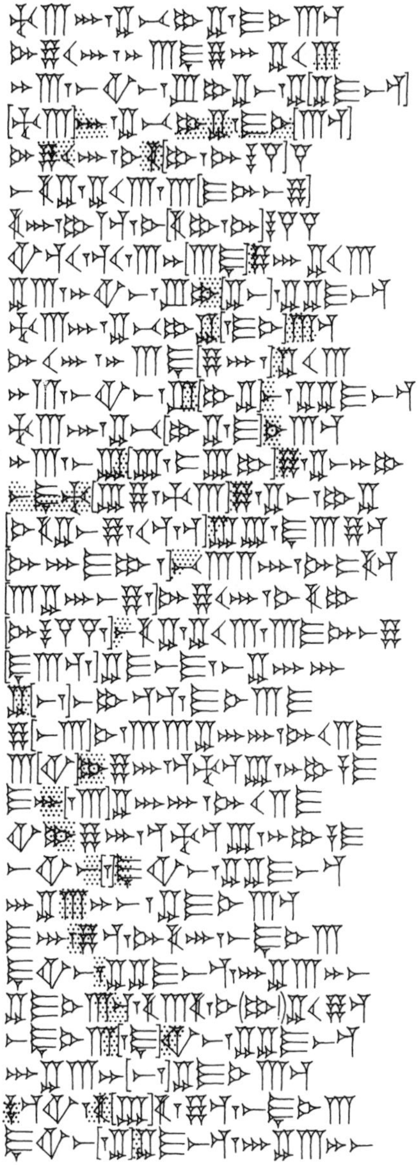

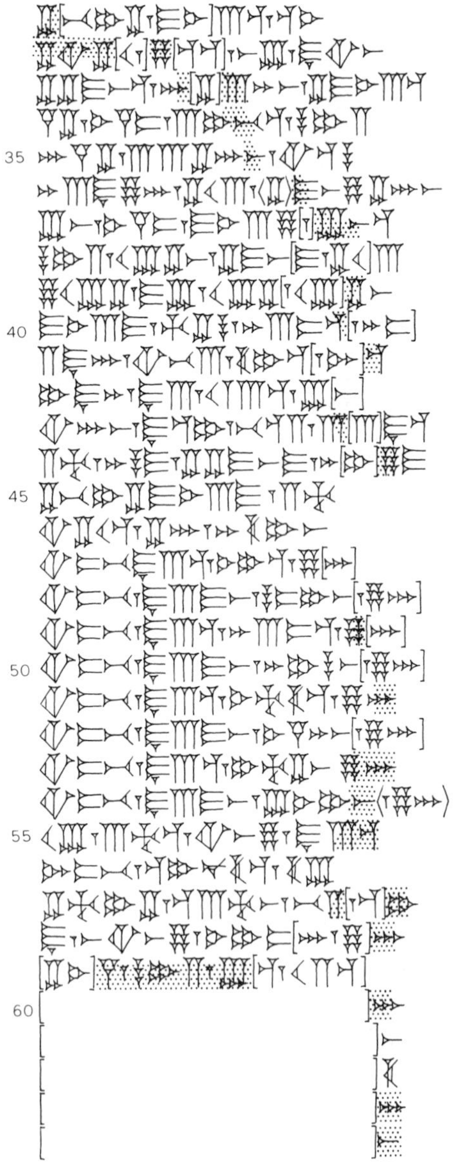

VII.1

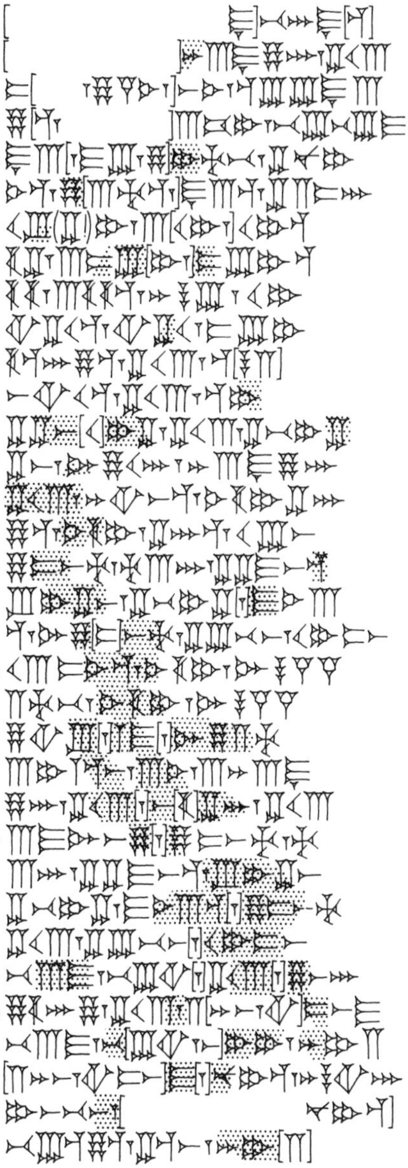

35 〔cuneiform〕

〔cuneiform〕

〔cuneiform〕

〔cuneiform〕

〔cuneiform〕

40 〔cuneiform〕

〔cuneiform〕

〔cuneiform〕

〔cuneiform〕

〔cuneiform〕

45 〔cuneiform〕

〔cuneiform〕

〔cuneiform〕

〔cuneiform〕

〔cuneiform〕

50 〔cuneiform〕

〔cuneiform〕

〔cuneiform〕

〔cuneiform〕

〔cuneiform〕

55 〔cuneiform〕

〔cuneiform〕

〔cuneiform〕

〔cuneiform〕

〔cuneiform〕

60 〔cuneiform〕

〔cuneiform〕

〔cuneiform〕

(broken)

VIII.1 〔cuneiform〕

〔cuneiform〕

〔cuneiform〕

〔cuneiform〕

5 〔cuneiform〕

10

15

20

25

30

35

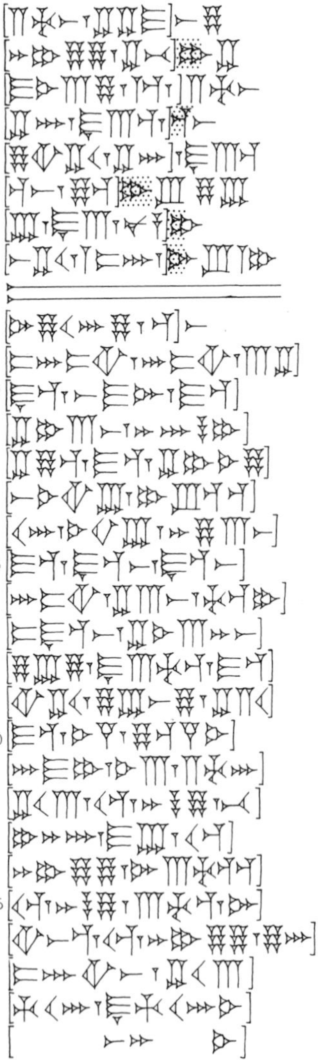

edge:

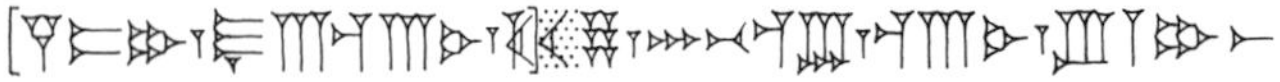

KTU 1.5

35 [cuneiform]

(broken)

II.1 [cuneiform]

5 [cuneiform]

10 [cuneiform]

15 [cuneiform]

20 [cuneiform]

25 [cuneiform]

(broken)

III.1 [cuneiform]

5
6
7
8
9
10
11
12
13
14
15
16
17
18
19
20
21
22
23
24
25
26
27
28
29

(broken)

IV.1
2
3
4
5
6
7
8

10

15

20

25

(broken)

V.

1

5

10

15 𒀭 ...

(cuneiform text, lines 15–25)

(broken)

VI.1ᵃ [...]
1ᵇ [...]
1ᶜ [...]

1 ...

5 ...

10 ...

15 ...

20

25

30

KTU 1.6

I.1

5

10

15

20

25

30

35

40

45

50

55

60

65

II.1

5

10

15

20

25

30

35

(broken)

III.1⁸

1

5

10

15

20

IV.1

5

10

15

20

25

(broken)

V.1*

1

5

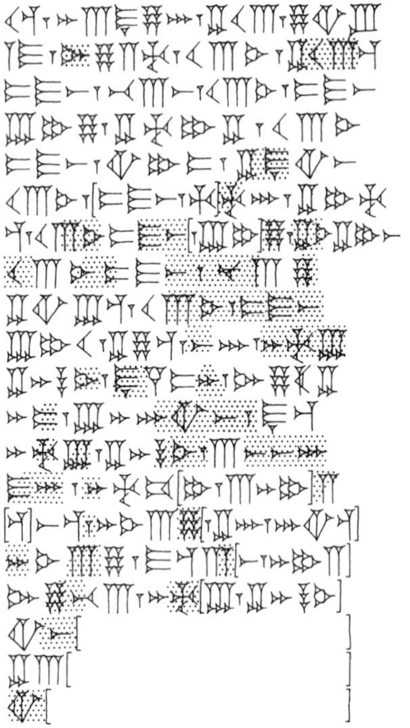

10 〈𒀭𒐊𒈨𒌍𒌍𒌍𒅗𒐊𒐊〈𒐊𒐊𒐊𒅗𒊑𒀭𒐊𒌍

𒐊𒌍𒀭𒀭𒐊𒊩𒐊𒊑〈𒐊𒐊𒈨𒀸𒐊𒐊𒈨𒐊

𒌍𒀸𒐊𒐊𒐊𒐊𒌍𒊑〈𒌍𒀸𒐊𒌍𒐊

𒌍𒈨𒀸𒐊𒐊𒀭𒈨𒀭𒐊𒐊〈𒐊𒌍𒀸

𒌍𒀸𒐊𒐊𒐊𒀭𒐊𒀸𒐊𒐊𒐊𒀭𒐊

15 〈𒌍𒀸𒐊𒌍𒀸𒐊𒐊𒀭𒐊𒈨𒌍𒈨𒀭

𒐊𒐊〈𒌍𒀭𒐊𒀸𒐊𒐊𒐊𒌍𒀸𒐊𒌍𒌍𒀭𒀭𒐊

𒐊𒌍𒀸𒐊𒐊𒐊𒐊𒐊𒐊𒌍𒐊

𒌍𒐊𒌍𒐊〈𒐊𒌍𒀸𒐊𒐊𒀸

𒌍𒀸〈𒐊𒌍𒐊𒐊𒐊𒈨𒌍𒈨𒌍𒈀𒐊𒌍

20 𒌍𒈨𒐊𒀸𒐊𒐊𒐊𒈨𒐊𒀸𒐊𒐊𒐊𒀭𒐊𒌍

𒈨𒀸𒐊𒌍𒈨𒈨𒐊𒀭𒐊𒐊𒐊𒐊𒀭

𒈨𒐊𒌍𒀭𒌍𒈨𒀸𒐊𒐊𒌍𒈨𒈨𒐊

𒀸𒐊𒐊𒐊𒐊𒐊𒐊𒐈𒐊𒐊𒌍𒈨𒈨𒐊𒐊

[𒀭]𒐊𒐊𒐈𒈨𒐊𒐊𒌍𒐊𒌍𒈨𒈨𒈨𒀭𒐊

25 𒈨𒐊𒌍𒐊𒐊𒐊𒐊𒀭𒌍[𒐊𒈨𒐊𒌍]

𒐊𒈨𒐊𒌍𒐊𒈨𒐊𒌍𒌍𒐊𒈨𒐊]

𒀭𒐊]   ]

𒌍𒌍[   ]

𒀭𒐊]   ]

(broken)

VI.1 [𒐊𒐊𒈨𒌍𒀸

[𒌍𒀭𒈨𒀸𒀭𒐊𒌍𒐊𒐊𒐊𒐊𒈨𒀭𒐊𒀸

[𒌍𒐊𒐊𒐊𒐊𒐊𒐈〈𒌍𒈨𒌍

[𒌍𒈨𒐊𒐊𒐊𒐊�ੀ�ੀ�ੀ�Ā

5 [𒌍𒀸𒌍𒐊𒌍𒈨𒐈𒌍�Ā�Ā

[𒌍𒈨�𒌍�Ā�Ā�Ā�Ā𒌍�Ā�Ā

[𒀸�𒌍𒀸�Ā�Ā𒌍𒈨�Ā𒌍�Ā�Ā

[𒀸�Ā𒌍[�]𒀭𒌍〈�Ā�Ā𒌍�Ā

[�Ā〈�Ā�Ā�𒌍𒈨�Ā�Ā𒌍�Ā�Ā

10 �Ā�Ā�Ā�Ā�Ā�Ā�Ā�Ā�Ā〈𒌍

𒌍(𒀭)�Ā𒌍�Ā𒈨�Ā𒌍�Ā�Ā�Ā𒌍�Ā

�Ā�Ā〈�Ā�Ā〈𒌍�Ā𒌍�Ā�Ā

𒌍�Ā�Ā�Ā�Ā�Ā𒌍(𒌍)�Ā�Ā�Ā�Ā𒌍�Ā

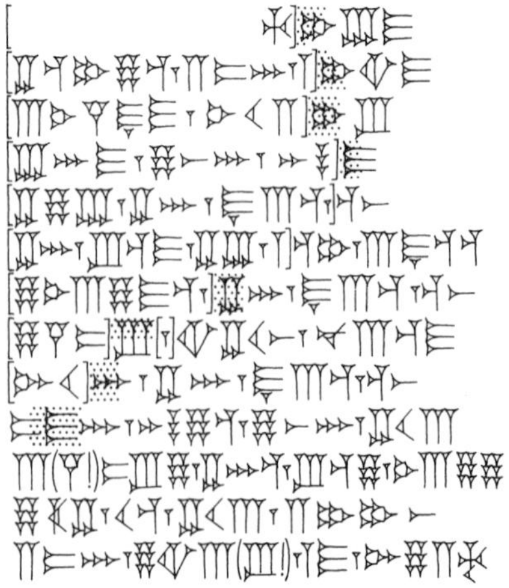

15 𒀭𒀭𒀭𒀭𒀭𒀭𒀭𒀭

20 𒀭𒀭𒀭𒀭𒀭𒀭

25 𒀭𒀭𒀭𒀭𒀭𒀭

30 𒀭𒀭𒀭𒀭𒀭𒀭

35 𒀭𒀭𒀭𒀭𒀭𒀭

40 𒀭𒀭𒀭𒀭𒀭𒀭

45 𒀭𒀭𒀭𒀭𒀭𒀭

50

55

KTU 1.96

1 𒀀 …

5 …

10 …

KTU 1.10

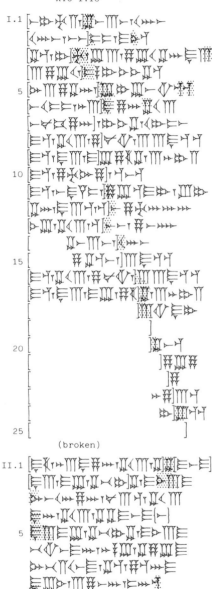

10

15

20

25

30

35

40

III.1

5

10

15

20

25

30

35

𒂼𒄩𒐖𒌋𒈫𒂼𒄩 𒐖𒑱𒂼𒂊
𒊏𒁾 𒄩𒈬𒐖𒂊𒌋𒊩𒂊𒈫

KTU 1.11

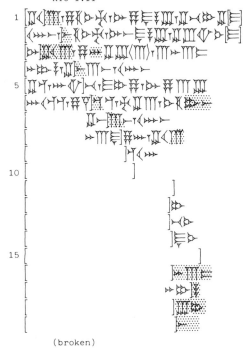

(broken)

KTU 1.23

1 𒀭𒁁𒌋𒀜𒈠𒐈𒁕𒁁𒋡𒁉𒁕𒑱]

𒁕𒉿𒅀𒁕𒋾𒌋𒈠𒊑𒑇𒋫𒀭]

𒐈𒌋𒈠𒁕𒑱𒁺𒁉𒑗𒈨𒐊𒌋𒈨𒍍𒀜𒐊𒋾𒑇𒐊𒀜𒌋𒁲

𒈨𒑗𒈨𒁕𒁉𒌋𒌋𒀜𒋾𒑗𒈨𒈠𒑇𒑗𒑖𒋾𒀜𒑇𒁹𒑗𒁺

5 𒈨𒁺𒍝𒌋𒑇𒋾𒁺𒀜𒑇𒌋𒑖 𒑖𒑱𒑇

𒈨𒑺𒑇𒀀𒈨𒐈𒑺𒑇𒋫𒌋𒀜𒑗𒀜𒑺𒌋𒑗𒀀𒑇𒀀𒋾𒐊𒁺𒀜𒑺𒈠𒈠𒑺

𒌋𒈨𒑖𒀀𒑺𒁺𒑗𒐈𒌋𒑇𒑺𒐈𒌋𒑺𒁺𒀜𒐊𒁁𒑖𒁹𒐊𒑺𒁺𒁇𒈠𒈠𒑇

———————————————————————————

𒑇𒁹𒁺𒌋𒁺𒑗𒌋𒅀𒑗𒑖𒑝𒑖𒋾𒑝𒑗𒁺𒑗𒋾𒑖𒍑

𒑇𒋾𒑗𒈨𒑇𒑇𒑺𒈠𒐊𒅀𒑖𒁺𒈠𒀜𒁹𒑖𒁺𒑗𒐊𒑺𒌋𒈠

10 𒅀𒑗𒈨𒈠𒈠𒑗𒑇𒐈𒑗𒑇𒐊𒁺𒈠𒑺𒅀𒌋𒀜𒑖𒌋𒑗𒑇𒍑

𒁺𒑇𒐊𒈠

———————————————————————————

𒌋𒑖𒀜𒑗𒁇𒑺𒑕𒑗𒀜𒑗𒑖𒀜𒑖𒁺𒀜𒁺𒑖𒑗𒀜𒈠𒅀𒑺

𒁺𒑗𒌋𒑖𒌋𒑖𒑱𒑖𒑇𒑗𒌋𒑖𒑺𒅀𒁺𒑗𒁺𒁺𒅀𒑗

𒀜𒑖𒑱𒌋𒑗𒌋𒑖𒀜𒑖𒑝𒅀𒁺𒑗𒑗𒀜𒑺𒐈𒑖𒑺𒑺𒅀𒑖𒑇𒑺𒑺

15 𒁺𒀜𒑖𒑖𒈠𒑗𒑺𒑗𒌋𒑖𒑖𒑖𒑗𒑇𒑖𒐈𒑺𒑺𒑕

𒑗𒑖𒁺𒑗𒑺𒅀𒑗𒑗𒁺𒑗𒑖𒑖𒑖𒑗𒑖𒀜𒍑]

𒑗𒑖𒑗𒁺𒑺𒑗𒑖𒑗𒑖𒑺𒑗𒀜𒑖𒑗𒌋𒁺𒑗𒀜𒑖𒍑]

𒌋𒑗𒑗𒑗𒀜𒁺𒑖𒑗𒑖𒑖𒑗]

𒑗𒑖𒑗𒑖𒑇𒑖𒑗𒑗𒑗𒑺𒑺𒑗𒑖𒑗𒑖𒑖𒑗𒑖𒑖𒑗𒑖𒑗]

20 𒑖𒑺𒑗𒑖𒌋𒑖𒑗

———————————————————————————

𒑖𒑗𒑺𒑖𒑗𒌋𒑗𒑖

𒑺𒑺𒑗𒌋𒁺𒑗𒑗

𒑖𒑗𒁺𒑺𒑺𒑖𒑖𒑗𒑗𒑺𒑗𒑗𒑺𒑗𒑗𒑖𒑖𒑺𒑗𒑖𒑗𒑗𒑖𒑗

𒑖𒑺𒑗𒑖𒑗𒑖𒑗𒑺𒑗𒑖𒑗𒑗𒑺𒑖𒑗𒑖𒑗𒑗]

25 𒌋𒑖𒌋𒑖𒑖𒑖𒑺𒑗𒑖𒑖𒑗𒑺𒑗[ ]

𒁺𒑗𒑺𒑖𒑗𒑗𒌋𒑖𒑗𒑖𒑺𒁺𒑗𒑗𒑖

𒑖𒑖𒁺𒑗𒑖𒑖𒑖𒑖𒑗𒑺𒑺𒑗𒑗

———————————————————————————

𒌋𒑖𒑖𒑖𒑗𒑗𒌋𒑖𒑗𒑺𒁺𒑗𒁺𒑗𒑺𒑗𒑖

𒑖𒑗𒑱𒑖𒁺𒑗𒑖𒑖

30 𒁺𒑖𒑖𒑗𒑕𒑖𒑗𒑖𒑖𒑺𒑗𒁺𒑖𒑖𒑖𒑗𒑗𒑖𒑺𒑗

𒁺𒑖𒑗𒑖𒑗𒑖𒑖𒑗𒌋𒑖𒑗𒑗𒑖𒑗𒑖𒑗𒑺𒌋𒑗𒑖𒑺

𒑖𒑖𒑗𒑖𒌋𒑖𒑖𒑗𒑖𒑖𒑗𒑖𒑺𒑖𒑗𒑖𒑗𒑺𒑖𒑗

𒁺𒑖𒑖𒑗𒑖𒑺𒑗𒑖𒑗𒑖𒑖𒑗𒑖𒑺𒁺𒑗𒑺𒑖𒑺𒑖𒑗𒑖𒑗

𒁺𒑗𒑖𒑖𒑗𒑖𒑗𒁺𒑗𒑖𒑖𒑗𒑖𒑺𒁺𒑗𒑖𒑖𒑗𒑖𒑺𒑗𒑖𒑺𒑗

35

40

45

50

55

60

65

70

75

KTU 1.12

I.1

5

10

15

20

25

30

35 𒀭𒀭𒀭

40

II.1 [   ]

5

10

15

20

25

30

35

40

45

50

55

60

KTU 1.114

1

5

10

15

20

25

30

KTU 1.13

1 [

5

10

15

20

25

30

(broken)

KTU 1.24

35 𒀭𒐊𒌋𒈠𒋫𒐊𒌍𒀀𒐊
𒌋𒁇𒀀𒌋𒈠𒑲𒄿𒈠𒈠𒐊𒐊𒈠
𒐉𒈠𒌋𒌋𒈠𒐊𒈠𒁇𒐉𒁇𒐊𒐉
𒐋𒈠𒀭𒁇𒐊𒁇𒀀𒐊𒀀𒑲𒐊𒀀
𒁇𒑲𒈠𒁇𒁇

40 𒈠𒀭𒁇𒐉𒐋𒀀𒁇𒐊𒁇𒐉𒈠
𒀀𒐊𒐋𒐋𒐊𒑲𒈠𒈠𒐋𒐉𒈠𒀀𒐊
𒐋𒐋𒐉𒐋𒐉𒐉𒐉𒐉𒐊𒁇𒁇𒐋𒀀
𒐉𒐋𒁇𒐉𒐉𒐉𒐊𒑲𒐉𒐊𒐉𒐋𒐉
𒐋𒐋𒈠𒐊𒐉𒐉𒐋𒐊𒀀𒈠𒐊

45 𒐋𒐋𒌋𒐊𒐋𒐊𒈠𒐉𒐊𒑲𒐊
𒁇𒐊𒈠𒐉𒐋𒐊𒀀𒐊𒀀𒈠𒐊𒈠
𒀀𒐊𒈠𒐋𒐉𒐊𒁇𒀀𒐋𒐉𒐊𒑲
𒑲𒀀𒈠𒀀𒐉𒐊𒐉𒐉𒀀𒀀𒀀
𒀀𒈠𒐉𒀀𒐉𒐉𒐊𒁇𒐉𒑲𒐋

50 𒐋𒌋𒈠𒀀𒐊𒐊𒁇𒀀𒁇𒐊𒐊𒁇𒀀

KTU 1.100

1 [cuneiform text]

5 [cuneiform text]

10 [cuneiform text]

15 [cuneiform text]

20 [cuneiform text]

25 [cuneiform text]

30 [cuneiform text]

* 34^a ⟨𒀭 cuneiform text ⟩
34^b cuneiform text
34^c cuneiform text
34^d cuneiform text
34^e cuneiform text ⟩

35 cuneiform text
cuneiform text
cuneiform text
cuneiform text
cuneiform text

40 cuneiform text
cuneiform text
cuneiform text
cuneiform text
cuneiform text

45 cuneiform text
cuneiform text
cuneiform text
cuneiform text
cuneiform text
50 cuneiform text

cuneiform text
cuneiform text
cuneiform text
cuneiform text
55 cuneiform text
cuneiform text

cuneiform text
cuneiform text
cuneiform text
60 cuneiform text
cuneiform text
cuneiform text
cuneiform text

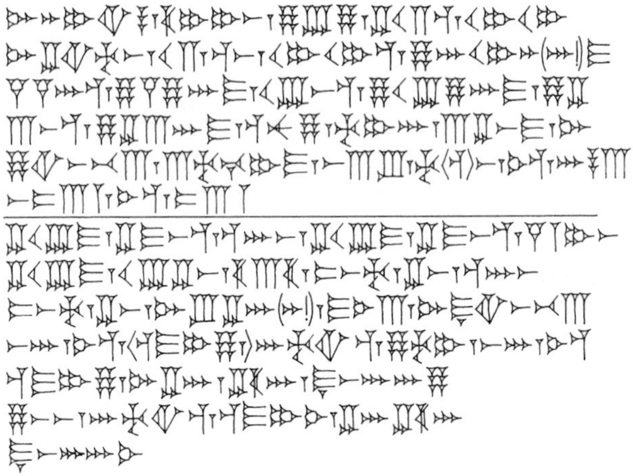

* Edge:

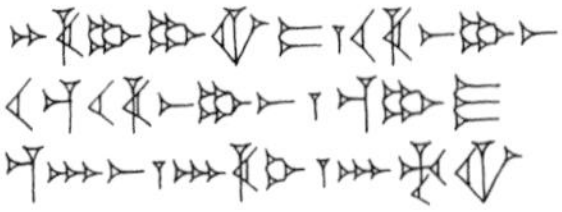

KTU 1.41

35

40

45

50

55

KTU 1.161

𒀭 𒈫 𒄭𒀀 𒀭 𒈫 𒄭𒀀 𒑖 𒁽 𒆠 [𒁲 𒌋]
𒁁 𒀭 𒈫 𒄭𒀀 𒈨 𒀀 (�- 𒈪) 𒇉 𒀭 𒈫 𒄭𒀀 𒐕𒁁 𒌋𒐊
𒀭 𒈫 𒄭𒀀 𒈨 𒁽 𒇉 𒀭 𒈫 𒄭𒀀 𒈪 𒁹 𒁁 𒀀
𒀭 𒈫 𒄭𒀀 𒐐 𒁁 𒇉

KTU 1.43

1

5

10

15

20

25

KTU 1.119

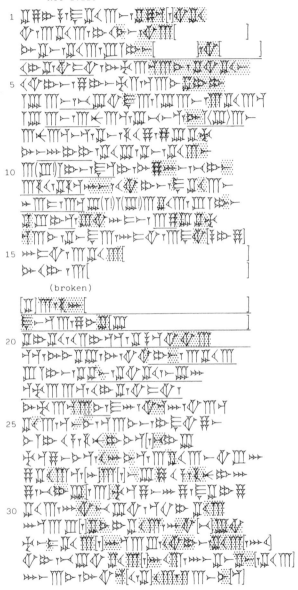

35 𒀀𒐈𒄀𒈫𒌋𒁉𒈫𒐈𒐏𒈣𒁕𒈨𒐈[𒁉𒈫𒁕𒐈]
𒈫𒌑𒅅𒀀𒈠𒁕𒈫

KTU 1.82

(broken)

KTU 1.82 Rs.

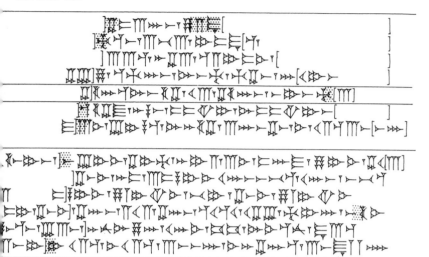

KTU 1.83

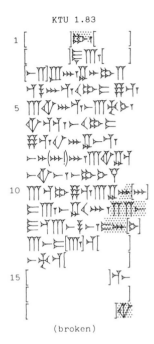

(broken)

RIH 78/20

1 𒀭𒀭𒀭 ...
2 ...
3 ...
4 ...
5 ...
6 ...
7 ...
8 ...
9 ...
10 ...
11 ...
12 ...
13 ...
14 ...
15 ...
16 ...
17 ...
18 ...
19 ...
20 ...

(broken)

KTU 1.93

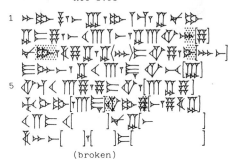

(broken)

KTU 1.108

KTU 1.14

I.1

5

10

15

20

25

30 [cuneiform]

[cuneiform]

[cuneiform]

[cuneiform]

[cuneiform]

35 [cuneiform]

[cuneiform]

[cuneiform]

[cuneiform]

[cuneiform]

40 [cuneiform]

[cuneiform]

[cuneiform]

[cuneiform]

[

45 [cuneiform]

[cuneiform]

[cuneiform]

[cuneiform]

[cuneiform]

50 [cuneiform]

[cuneiform]

[cuneiform]

II.1 [cuneiform]

[cuneiform]

[cuneiform]

[cuneiform]

5 [cuneiform]

[cuneiform]

10

15

20

25

30

35

40

45

50

III.1

5

10

15

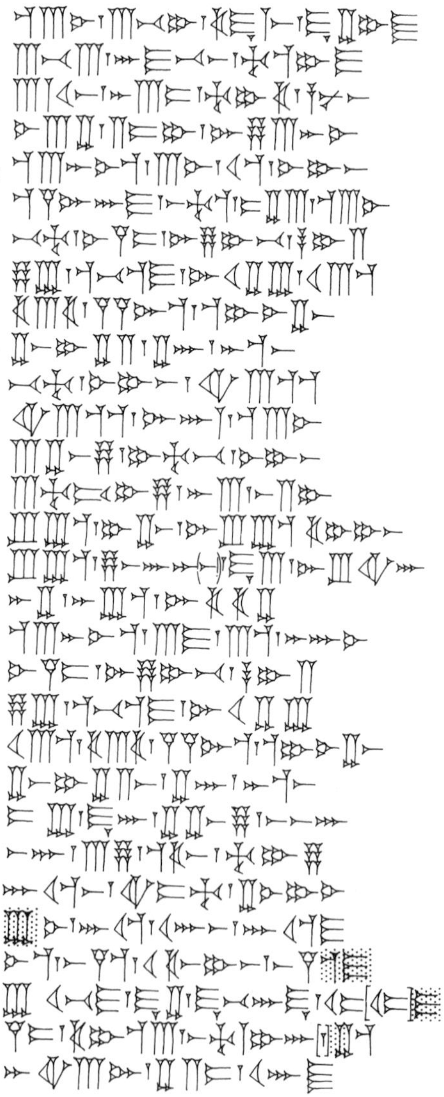

50

55

IV.1

5

10

15

20

25

30

35

40

45

50

V.1

5

10

15

20

25

30

35

40

45

VI.1ᵃ

1ᵇ

1ᶜ

1

5

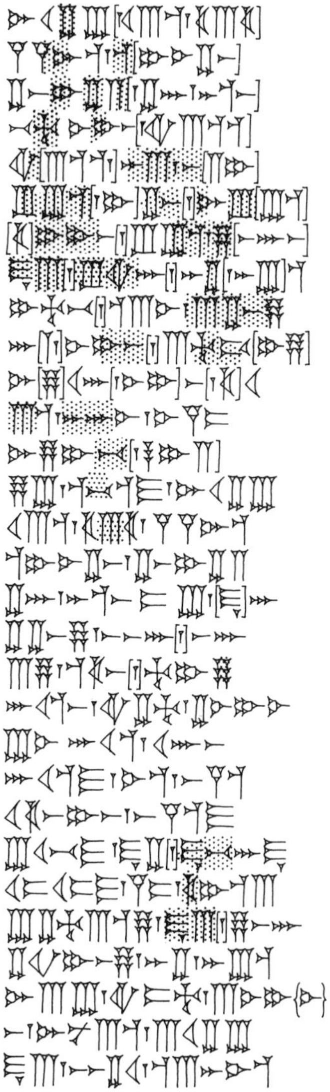

𒈨𒊹𒐊𒌷𒈨𒊑𒈨𒌋
𒈨𒊹𒌋𒐊𒌋𒐊𒌋𒈨𒐊𒈨
𒈪𒌋𒐊𒌋𒐊𒌋𒌋
𒐊𒐊𒐊𒌋𒐊𒈨𒐊𒌋
40 𒌋𒌋𒐊𒐊𒌋𒐊𒌋𒐊𒌋[𒌋]
𒐊𒌋𒐊[𒌋]𒐊𒌋[𒐊𒌋𒈨𒌋]
[𒐊 𒈨   ]

KTU 1.15

I.1* [𒅑 ⯈ ⯈ ⊢]

[⫶ 𒅑 ⋅ 𒅑 ⊣ ⯈ ⯈ ⯈ ⯈ ⊢ ⯈ ⊢ ⯈ ▽ ⊢]

[⯈ ⯈ ⯈ ⊢ ⟨ ⊢ ⯈ ⯈ 𒅑]

[⯈ 𒅑 ⋅ ⊣ ⟨ ⊣ ⫶ ⊢ ⟨ 𒅑 𒅑]

5* [⟨ 𒅑 ⊣ ⟨ 𒅑 ⟨ ⋅ ▽ ▽ ⯈ ⊣]

[⊣ ⯈ ⯈ 𒅑 ⊢ ⋅ 𒅑 ⊢ ⯈ 𒅑 𒅑]

[𒅑 ⯈ ⋅ ⊢ ⊣ ⊢ ⋅ ⊢ 𒅑 ⫶ ⯈]

[𒅑 𒅑 ⊢ ⊣ ⊢ ⊢ ⯈ ⊢ ⊢]

[𒅑 ⊣ ⋅ ⊣ ⟨ ⊢ ⋅ ⊢ ⯈ ⊣]

10* [⯈ ⟨ ⊣ ⊢ ⋅ ⟨ 𒅑 ⟨ 𒅑 ⯈ ⯈ ⯈]

[𒅑 ⯈ ⯈ ⟨ ⊣ ⟨ ⯈ ⊢]

[⯈ ⟨ ⊣ ⫶ ⊢ ⯈ ⊣ ⊢ ▽ ⊣]

[⟨ ⟨ ⊢ ⯈ ⊢ ⊢ ▽ ⊣ ⫶]

[𒅑 ⟨ ⊣ ⫶ ⫶ 𒅑 ⫶ ⊣ ⟨ ⯈ ⫶]

15* [⟨ ⊢ ⟨ ⊢ ⫶ ▽ ⊢ ⟨ ⯈ ⊣ 𒅑]

[𒅑 𒅑 ⊣ ⟨ 𒅑 ⊣ ⟨ ⫶ 𒅑 ⊢ ⯈]

[𒅑 ⟨ ⯈ ⊢ ⊣ ⊢ 𒅑 ⊢ 𒅑 ⊣]

[⯈ 𒅑 𒅑 ⋅ ⟨ ⯈ ⊢ ⟨ 𒅑 ⯈ ⯈ ⊢]

[⯈ ⊢ ⟨ 𒅑 ⊣ 𒅑 ⟨ 𒅑 𒅑]

20* [⫶ 𒅑 ⯈ ⊣ ⟨ ⊢ ⫶ 𒅑 𒅑]

[⊣ 𒅑 ⯈ ⋅   ]

(broken)

II. 1 [⊣ ⯈ ⊣ ⟨ 𒅑 ⊣ 𒅑 ⟨ ⯈ ⯈ ░░░░░

⊣ ⟨ ⟨ ⊢ ⊣ ⟨ ⊣ ⊣ 𒅑 ⟨ ⯈ ⊢

⊢ ⟨ ⟨ ⯈ ⯈ ⯈ ⊣ 𒅑 ⯈ ⟨ 𒅑 𒅑 ⯈

⟨ ⊣ ⯈ ⯈ ⊢ ⊢ ⫶ ▽ ⯈ ⯈ ⫶

5 ⯈ ⯈ ⫶ ⊢ ⊣ ⋅ ⫶ ⊢ 𒅑 ⟨ ⫶ ⫶

𒅑 ⯈ ⫶ ⟨ ⟨ 𒅑 𒅑 ⊣ ⊣ ⟨ ⊣

⯈ ⊢ ⯈ ⟨ ⯈ ⊢ 𒅑 𒅑 ⊣ ⊣

⯈ ⫶ ⟨ ⯈ ⫶ ⯈ ⯈ ⯈ ⊢ ⟨ ⟨

⊢⊢]

II   (broken)

1

5

10

15

20

25

III   (broken)

1

5 [cuneiform]

[cuneiform]

[cuneiform]

[cuneiform]

[cuneiform]

10 [cuneiform]

[cuneiform]

[cuneiform]

[cuneiform]

[cuneiform]

15 [cuneiform]

[cuneiform]

[cuneiform]

[cuneiform]

[cuneiform]

20 [cuneiform]

[cuneiform]

[cuneiform]

[cuneiform]

[cuneiform]

25 [cuneiform]

[cuneiform]

[cuneiform]

[cuneiform]

[cuneiform]

30 [cuneiform]

[cuneiform]

(broken)

IV   (broken)

1 [cuneiform]

[cuneiform]

[cuneiform]

[cuneiform]

5 [cuneiform]

10

15

20

25

(broken)

V   (broken)

1

5

10

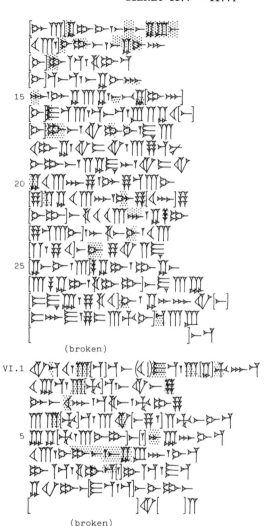

15

20

25

(broken)

VI.1

5

(broken)

KTU 1.16

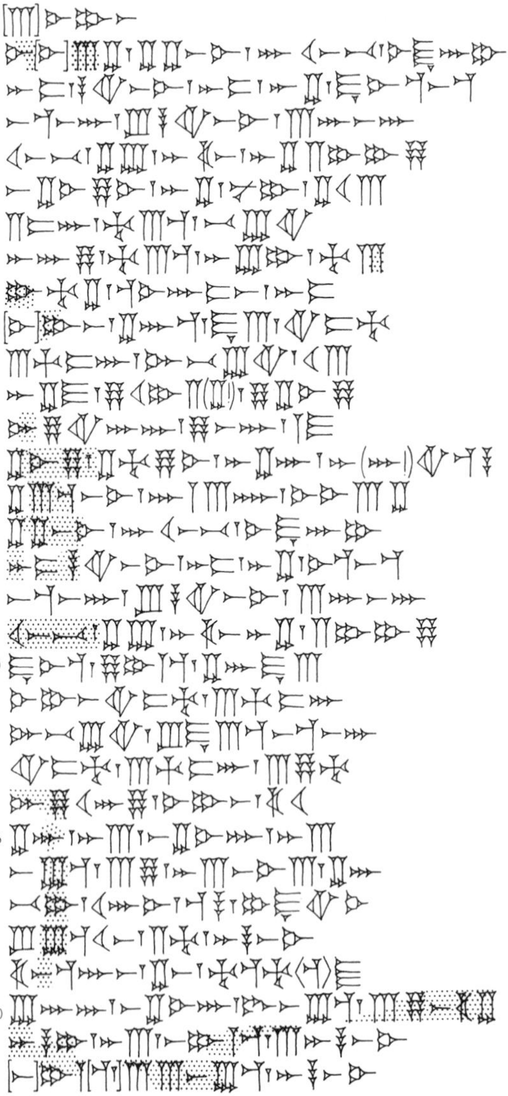

35

40

45

50

55

60

II.1

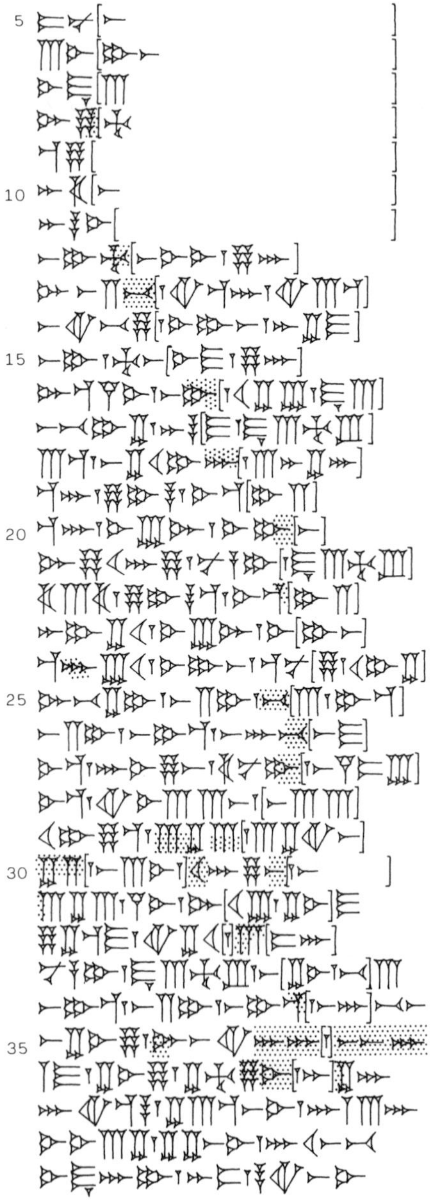

40 〔cuneiform〕

45 〔cuneiform〕

50 〔cuneiform〕

55 〔cuneiform〕

(broken)

III (broken)

1 〔cuneiform〕

5 〔cuneiform〕

10 〔cuneiform〕

15

(broken)

IV   (broken)

1

5

10

15

(broken)

V.1

5

10

15

20

25

30

35

40

(broken)

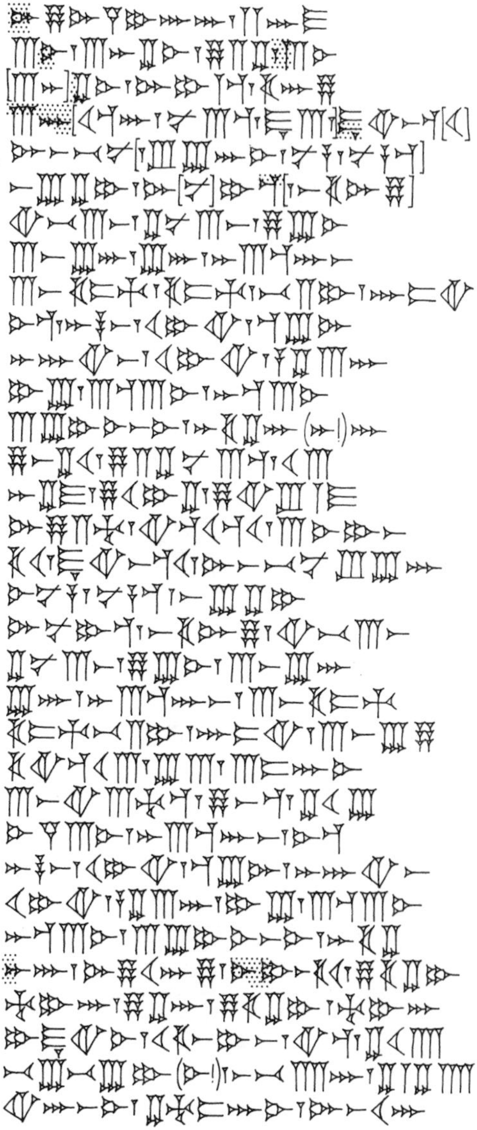

margo:

KTU 1.17

I.1*

1

5

10

15

20

25

30

35

40

45

50

(broken)

II.1a

1b

1c

1

5

10

15

20

25

30

35

40

---

* The scribe omitted

(cuneiform text)

45 (cuneiform text)

(broken)

V.1 (cuneiform text)

5 (cuneiform text)

10 (cuneiform text)

15 (cuneiform text)

20 (cuneiform text)

25 (cuneiform text)

30

35

(broken)

VI.1

5

10

15

20

(broken)

KTU 1.18

(broken)

IV.1

5

10

15

20

25

30

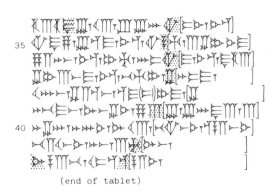

35

40

(end of tablet)

KTU 1.19

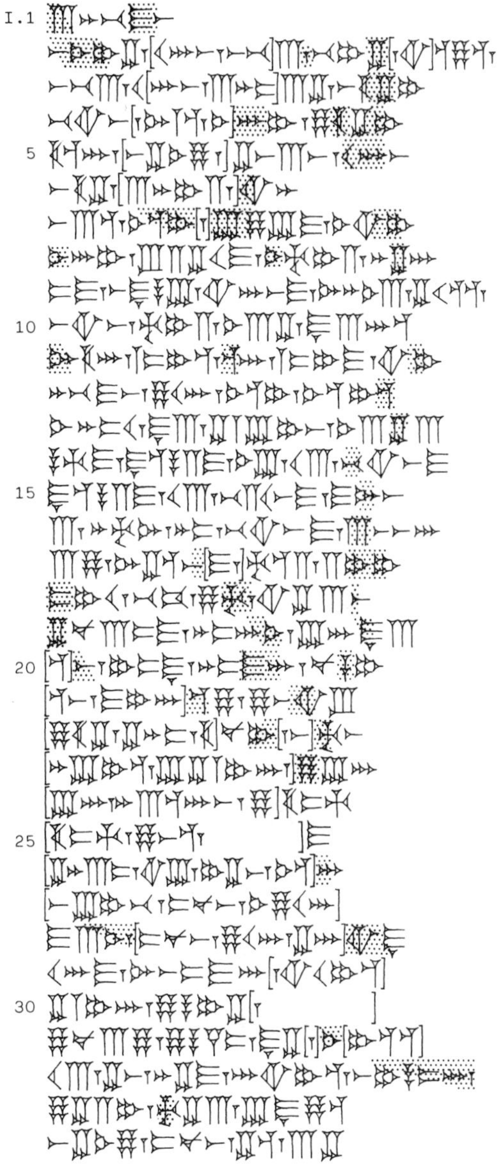

I.1 [cuneiform text]
[cuneiform text]
[cuneiform text]
[cuneiform text]
5 [cuneiform text]
[cuneiform text]
[cuneiform text]
[cuneiform text]
[cuneiform text]
10 [cuneiform text]
[cuneiform text]
[cuneiform text]
[cuneiform text]
[cuneiform text]
15 [cuneiform text]
[cuneiform text]
[cuneiform text]
[cuneiform text]
[cuneiform text]
20 [cuneiform text]
[cuneiform text]
[cuneiform text]
[cuneiform text]
[cuneiform text]
25 [cuneiform text]
[cuneiform text]
[cuneiform text]
[cuneiform text]
[cuneiform text]
30 [cuneiform text]
[cuneiform text]
[cuneiform text]
[cuneiform text]
[cuneiform text]

35

40

45

II.1

5

10

15

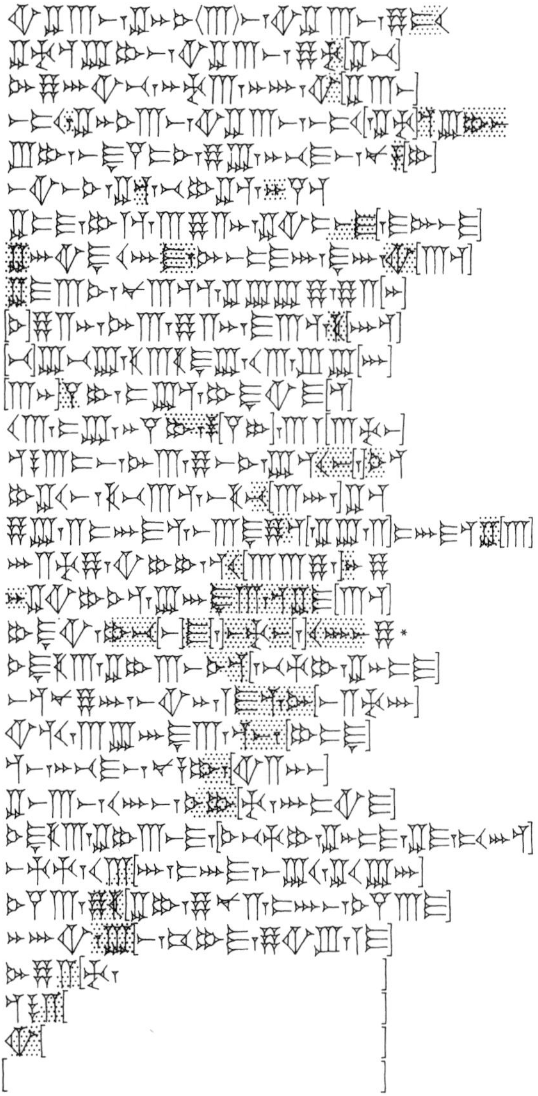

20 𒀭𒈨𒌍𒈠𒋾𒐉𒀭𒈨𒌍𒐌𒋾𒐉𒈨𒌍

[cuneiform text - lines 20-50 and marginal note]

55

III.1

5

10

15

20

25

30

35

40

45

50

55

IV.1

5

10

15

20

25

30

35

40

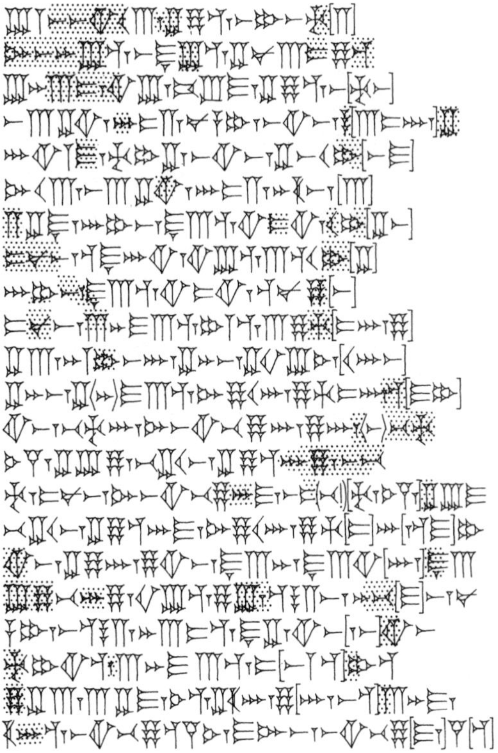

Edge, starting at the height of IV.23:

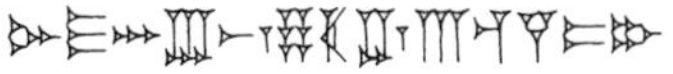

KTU 1.21

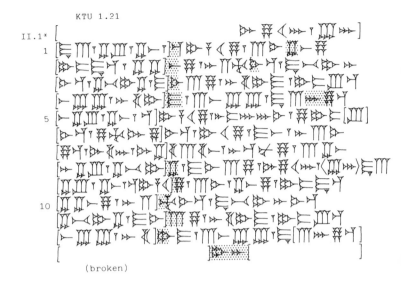

(broken)

KTU 1.20

(broken)

(broken)

KTU 1.22

III.1

5

10

15

20

25

(broken)

IV.1*

1

5

10

15

20

25

(broken)

CONVERSION TABLE KTU - CARTU

ALPHABETICAL GLOSSARY

With every separate lemma at least one reference is given.
The following abbreviations are used:

A = Aqhat   L = Loves
B = Baal   MR = Myth and Ritual
In = Incantation R = Ritual
K = Keret

ʾ

ʾab   father (B I.iv.54)
ʾabd   destruction, destructive venom (MR VI.5)
ʾabyn   poor (A. I.i.16)
ʾablm   Abiluma (city) (A II.i.27)
ʾabn   1. stone (B I.iii.22)
       2. deity (MR VI.1)
ʾagzr   eager (MR IV.29)
ʾagzry   ravenous (MR I.23)
ʾagn   fire-pan (MR I.15)
ʾad   father (MR I.32)
ʾadm   man(kind) (B I.ii.8)
ʾadn   1. lord (B I.v.9)
       2. father (MR V.33)
ʾadr   mighty (A I.v.7)
ʾadr   see ʾdr
ʾadt   mistress (B I.vi.24)

ʾaḥbt   love, passion (B I.iii.7)
ʾaḥl   tent (A I.v.32)
ʾazmr   cut foliage (R I.51)
ʾaḥd   one, alone (B III.i.25)
ʾaḥdh   together (MR III.31)
ʾaḥl   see ḥly
ʾaḥ   brother (B VI.ii.12)
ʾaḥ   shore (L II.ii.9)
ʾaḥr   1. after (MR V.32)
       2. backwards (K III.i.31)
       3. afterwards (B III.i.30)
ʾaḥt   sister (B I.iv.39)
ʾay   whatever (A I.vi.2)
ʾayl   hart (B VI.i.24)
ʾaylt   doe (B II.v.19)

ʾaymr   Ayyamur, name of magic weapon (B III.i.6)

ʾakl   food (K I.ii.28)

ʾakl   devourer, monster (MR II.i.26)

ʾakl   decay (A III.i.9)

ʾaklt   fissured land (A III.ii. 19)

ʾal   1. not (prohibitive) (B I.i.1)
   2. surely

ʾal   mantle (A III.i.37)

ʾal   fine sheep (In I.8)

ʾalʾiy   very mighty (B I.iii. 14)

ʾalʾiyn   almighty (B I.i.2)

ʾall   mantle (B VI.ii.11)

ʾalmnt   widow (A I.v.8)

ʾaln   plain (MR II.i.20)

ʾalp   ox (B I.iv.41)

ʾalp   thousand (B I.i.15)

ʾalt   door-jamb (B III.iii.17)

ʾalt   sworn obligation (In I.2)

ʾamd   always (A III.iii.47)

ʾamht   pl. of ʾamt

ʾamr   Amurru (country) (B IV.i.41)

ʾamr   speech (B III.i.15)

ʾamrr   Amruru (god) (B III. vi.11)

ʾamt   1. forearm (K I.ii.10)
   2. cubit (B V.i.6)

ʾamt   handmaid (B IV.iii. 21)

ʾan   I (pers.pron.) (B I.iv. 22)

ʾan   this (dem.pron.) (B VI. iv.22)

ʾan   strength (B VI.i.50)

ʾanhb   murex(-dye) (B I.ii.3)

ʾanḫr   sperm-whale (B IV. viii.50)

ʾank   I (pers.pron.) (B I.iii. 28)

ʾannḫ   mint (MR I.14)

ʾanpn   nose, face (MR II.ii. 37)

ʾanš   small of the back (B I.iii.35)

ʾanš   companion (K III.vi. 36)

ʾanšt   friendliness (A II.iv. 10)

ʾanšt   fem. inf. D ʾnš

ʾasm   granary (A III.ii.18)

ʾasr   band (A III.ii.32)

ʾasr   prisoner (B III.i.37)

ʾaġzt   protection-marriage (MR V.3)

ʾap   1. nose, beak (B III.i. 13)

2. tip, point, nipple (MR I.24)

3. prime (time) (B IV.v.6)

4. front, entrance (B I.v.11)

5. anger, fury (B III.i.38)

ʾap   alas! (A II.iv.26)

ʾap   then, also (B I.iv.31)

ʾaphn   thereat (A I.i.1)

ʾaplb   breast (B V.vi.21)

ʾapn   then, also (B I.i.24)

ʾapnk   then, also (A I.ii.27)

ʾaps   edge, top of chair (B VI.i.61)

ʾapᶜ   viper (A III.i.13)

ʾapq   bedding (B I.v.6)

ʾar   honey-like dew (B I.i.24)

ʾarbdd   tranquillity (B I.iii.17)

ʾarbᶜ   four (K III.ii.23)

ʾargmn   tribute (purple?) (R 1.4)

ʾarz   cedar (B IV.v.10)

ʾarḫ   ox, cow (B VI.i.6)

ʾarḫt   cow (B IV.vi.50)

ʾary   kin, family (B I.v.37)

ʾarkt   long arm (B I.v.23)

ʾarṣ   1. earth, land (B I.i.4)

2. goddess Earth (In I.38)

ʾarṣy   Arsayu (goddess) (B I.iv.51)

ʾarr   Araru (mountain) (L II.iii.11)

ʾarš   Arishu (monster) (B I.iii.43)

ʾaršḫ   Arashikh (river) (MR VI.63)

ʾaškrr   henbane (MR III.15)

ʾat   you (pers. pron.) (B I.iii.28)

ʾatm   you (pl. pers.pron.) (B I.iv.33)

ʾatn   Attanu (PN) (B VI.vi.55)

ʾatnt   donkey (B IV.iv.7)

ʾaṯr   holy place (A I.i.28)

ʾaṯr   after (B VI.ii.9)

ʾaṯryt   future (A I.vi.36)

ʾaṯrt   Athiratu (goddess) (B I.i.15)

ʾaṯt   married woman (B I.i.14)

ʾi   where? (B V.iv.6)

ʾi   woe! (K III.i.3)

ʾi   as surely as (K I.iv.38)

ʾi   island (B I.vi.8)

ʾib 1. blossom (A III.i.31)
     2. Ibbu (goddess)
        (MR V.1)
ʾib pure (K I.iii.43)
ʾib enemy (B I.iii.37)
ʾibᶜlt month name (R IV.1)
ʾibr bull (L II.iii.20)
ʾibr feathers (B IV.vii.56)
ʾid then (R I.50)
ʾidk thereupon (B I.iv.37)
ʾidm redness (MR II.ii.29)
ʾidt obligation (K II.iii.30)
ʾiht pl. of ʾi island
ʾiy where? (B VI.iv.4)
ʾik 1. why? (B I.iii.36)
     2. how? (B VI.vi.26)
ʾil 1. god, divine (B Ia.2)
     2. mighty (A III.i.13)
     3. Ilu (god) (B I.v.7)
ʾil ram (B II.iv.31)
ʾilʾib 1. Ilʾibu (god) (R I.
        35)
     2. ancestral god (A I.
        i.26)
ʾilh Ilahu (god) (In V.13)
ʾilhm Ilahuma (gods)
       (R I.6)
ʾilht pl. of ʾilt
ʾilḫʾu Iluhaʾu (PN) (K III.
        i.46)
ʾill weakness (B V.v.16)

ʾilmlk Ilimilku (PN) (B VI.
        vi.54)
ʾiln old tree (A III.i.10)
ʾilny ghost (B VI.vi.47)
ʾilqṣ nugget (B IV.v.17)
ʾilš Ilishu (god) (K III.iv.3)
ʾilt goddess (B I.ii.18)
ʾim if, whether (B VI.v.21)
ʾimr sheep, lamb (B I.v.1)
ʾimt truly, indeed (B IV.
      viii.55)
ʾin there is not (B I.iv.47a)
ʾinbb Inbubu (mountain)
       (B I.iv.34)
ʾinr puppy, young dog
      (K III.i.2)
ʾinš friendly (B VI.vi.41)
ʾipʾu drizzle (L II.ii.32)
ʾipd cloak (B V.i.5)
ʾiṣr store-house (B Ia.4)
ʾiqnʾu 1. lapis-lazuli (B II.
         ii.5)
     2. blue (MR I.21)
ʾirby locust (B I.ii.10)
ʾirt 1. breast (B I.iii.5)
     2. flank (A IVc.iv.25)
ʾiš fire (MR II.i.10)
ʾišd leg, foundation (B Ia.6)
ʾišḫry Ishkhariyu (goddess)
        (R IV.14)
ʾišqb leg (B II.v.19)

ʾišryt   happiness (A II.i.28)

ʾišt   1. fire (B III.i.32)
         2. Ishatu (monster)
            (B I.iii.45)

ʾitml   yesterday (R IV.19)

ʾitnn   present for love
         (MR VI.74)

ʾiṯ   there is, exist (B Ia.8)

ʾiṯl   spittle (B II.ii.9)

ʾiṯm   fleshy animal (B V.iii.
         24)

ʾu   1. and (In III.5)
       2. or (B III.iii.11)

ʾu   woe! (A II.iv.26)

ʾugr   brick (MR II.i.25)

ʾugr   see gpn

ʾugrt   Ugarit (city, kingdom)
         (In V.26)

ʾudm   1. Udumu (city) (K I.
            iii.4)
         2. Udumite (K II.i.
            17)

ʾudmᶜ   tear (B VI.i.10)

ʾudn   1. ear (A II.iv.23)
         2. aerie (B I.iv.2)

ʾudr   slope (B IV.v.17)

ʾuzᶜrt   hairless spot (B Ia.6)

ʾuzr   oblation (A I.i.2)

ʾuḫry   end, tip (A III.iii.49)

ʾuḫryt   end, future (A I.vi.
         35)

ʾuṭ   span (B III.i.13)

ʾul   strength, force (B III.
         iv.5)

ʾulkn   Ulikenu (PN, spirit)
         (R II.4)

ʾulmn   widowerhood (MR
         I.9)

ʾulṯ   brick-mould (B IV.iv.
         60)

ʾum   mother (B VI.vi.6)

ʾumht   pl. of ʾum

ʾumt   family (B VI.iv.19)

ʾun   mourning (B V.vi.15)

ʾun   1. strength (B V.ii.22)
       2. spell, magic (A III.
            i.40)

ʾuġr   Ughra (mountain)
         (B I.iv.34)

ʾupqt   stream-bed (B II.v.
         11)

ʾuṣbᶜ   finger (A III.i.7)

ʾuṣbᶜt   finger (B I.ii.32)

ʾur   herb, greenery (B I.iii.
         3a)

ʾurbt   lattice (B IV.v.61)

ʾušk   testicle (L III.2)

ʾušn   present (K I.iii.31)

ʾušpġt   neck-piece (R III.4)

ʾuṯkl   bunch of grapes
         (R 1.2)

ʾbd   G perish (B III.iv.3)
       Gt be destroyed
          (K I.i.8)

ʾg   G murmur (In I.43)

ʾgg   see ʾg

ʾgr   G hire (A III.iv.51)

ʾdy   G fulfil an obligation (In I.2)

ʾdm   D apply rouge (A III.iv.42)

　　N 1. make oneself red (A III.iv.42)

　　2. ruddy oneself, scrub (K I.ii.9)

ʾdr   G be mighty (A I.vi.20)

ʾhb   G love (B V.v.18)

ʾwl   see ʾl

ʾwr   see ʾr

ʾzr   G tie up (In I.13)

ʾḫd   G 1. grasp, take, seize (B I.iii.3)

　　2. cover (B III.iii.10)

　　N be seized (A III.i.9)

ʾḫd   see ʾḫd

ʾḫr   G follow (B III.i.47)

ʾkl   G consume (B IV.vi.24)

　　N be consumed (MR II.ii.13)

ʾl   D give strength (MR II.ii.56)

ʾml   Lp wilt (B III.i.43)

ʾmṣ   G be strong (In I.14)

ʾmr   G see (B III.iv.2)

Gt 1. regard (B I.i.22)

　　2. appear, look like (B III.i.32)

　　N be seen (In I.15)

ʾmr   G say (B III.i.15)

ʾnḫ   G sigh (A I.i.17)

ʾny   G groan (B I.v.35)

ʾnš   G be like a man (B I.v.27)

　　D make a companion (B III.i.38)

ʾsp   G rather in, collect (A III.ii.17)

　　Gp be gathered (B II.iv.11)

　　Gt gather in (K I.i.18)

ʾsr   G bind (B II.ii.7)

　　Gp be bound (A III.ii.31)

ʾpy   G bake (K I.ii.30)

ʾpq   D let flow freely (In III.12)

ʾr   G shine upon (L II.ii.20)

ʾrḥ   G travel (A I.i.38)

ʾrk   G be long (MR I.33)

ʾrš   G ask, wish (B I.v.28)

ʾtw   see ʾty

ʾty   G come (B I.iv.33)

ʾtr   G follow (B IV.iv.18)

b

b   in, on, with, from, as (B Ia.2)

b ʾ   G enter (B I.v.7)

b ʾir   well, metaph. vulva (MR IV.25)

bbt   Bibitu (city) (MR VI.31)

bd   dirge (K III.i.5)

bd   *b* + *yd* (B I.i.10)

bddy   alone (A III.ii.28)

bdy   G improvise (B I.i.18)

bdq   slit (MR IV.32)

bdqt   rift (B IV.vii.19)

bhm   G be cattle (MR II.i.5)

bht   pl. of *bt*: mansion (B I.ii.4)

bẖṯ   G hasten to meet (B V.ii.11)

bwʾ   see *bʾ*

bwš   see *bš*

bwṯ   see *bṯ*

bẖr   young man (K II.v.5)

bṯn   belly (MR II.ii.41)

by   I beg you, pray (B III.iii.19)

byn   see *bn*

bk   weeping (B VI.i.9)

bk   goblet (B I.i.12)

bky   G weep, bewail (B VI.i.16)

N weep (R II.13)

bkl   confusion (In I.26)

bkm   thereupon, then (B IV.vii.42)

bkr   first-born (K I.iii.40)

bkr   D make a first-born (K II.iii.16)

bl   not, surely (A I.i.20)

bl   without (A III.i.44)

bly   D devour (B IV.viii.56)

blmt   immortality (A I.vi.27)

blʿ   G swallow (R II.16)

blt   not, surely (B VI.i.54)

bm   see *b*

bmt   thorax, back, height (B I.ii.12)

bn   between (B Ia.5)

bn   G 1. understand (B I.iii.26)

     2. pay attention (In I.3)

     Lt observe intently (In III.17)

bn   son, child (B I.v.18)

bnw   pass. part. of *bny*

bnwn   building (K III.iv.13)

bny   G 1. build (B II.iii.7)

     2. create, beget (B IV.ii.11)

bnt   1. creation (A I.vi.13)

     2. growth, crop (MR II.ii.43)

bnt   pl. of *bt*

bᶜd   1. behind (K III.vi.49)
    2. for (MR I.70)

bᶜdn   behind (B I.iii.32)

bᶜl   1. lord, master (B VI.
    vi.58)
    2. Baᶜlu (god) (B Ia.1)

bᶜl   G make (A I.vi.24)

bᶜlt   mistress (R I.5)

bᶜr   D bring (K I.ii.48)
    S lead (B IV.iv.16)

bᶜr   D kindle (B I.iv.26)

bġy   G ask, beg (B I.iii.29)

bṣ   linen (K III.ii.30)

bṣql   bulging green ear of
    grain (A III.ii.13)

bṣr   G espy, watch (A II.iv.
    20)

bqᶜ   G split (B VI.ii.32)

bqᶜt   Baqiᶜatu (goddess)
    (MR V.48)

bqr   see *mqr*

bqṯ   D seek (B VI.iv.20)

br   cistern (B VI.ii.4)

br   electrum (B IV.i.35)

brd   G/D cut (B I.i.6)

brḥ   G flee (B V.i.1)

brk   Gp be blessed (A III.iv.
    32)
    D bless (A I.i.23)

brk   knee (B I.ii.13)

brk   L crouch (MR II.i.26)

brky   pool (B IV.viii.52)

brlt   1. throat (K III.i.42)
    2. life (B II.ii.10)
    3. pleasure (B IV.viii.
    52)

brq   lightning (B Ia.3)

brr   pure, clean (R I.3)

brt   covenant (B I.i.28)

bš   G depart (B I.iv.33)

bšr   D bring good news
    (A III.ii.37)
    Dp receive good news
    (B IV.v.26)

bšr   1. flesh, meat
    (B IV.ii.5)
    2. metaph. penis
    (MR V.9)

bšrt   good news (B IV.v.27)

bt   house (B I.ii.4)

bt   daughter (B I.iii.46)

btl   Gp be deflowered (L II.
    iii.9)

btlt   virgin (B I.ii.32)

bṯ   G be ashamed (B III.iv.
    28)

bṯy   G flatter (L I.6)

bṯn   male serpent (B I.iii.41)

bṯnt   female serpent (In I.35)

bṯt   1. shamefulness (B IV.
    iii.19)
    2. shameful act (B II.
    iv.5)

g

g   voice (B I.iii.36)

g²an   presumption (A I.vi. 44)

gb   1. back, crest (B II.v.13)
      2. top of tree (MR V.43)

gb   cistern (R III.1)

gbl   height, peak (B III.i.9)

gbl   Byblos (city) (B I.vi.7)

gbᶜ   hill (B I.iii.31)

gbṭṭ   hump (MR II.i.31)

gg   roof (A I.i.32)

ggn   pipe, gullet, soul (K III.vi.26)

ggt   roof (K I.ii.27)

gd   sinew (A I.vi.21)

gd   coriander (B I.ii.2)

gdl   great (B I.v.12)

gdlt   large female cattle, cow (R I.12)

gdlt   greatness (B I.v.23)

gdrt   stone wall (A III.i.13)

gwl   see *gl*

gzr   ravenous, eager (MR I. 63)

gḫṭ   G throw out (In III.1)

gyl   see *gl*

gl   G exult, cry out (K III. i.15)
      D make cry out (In I.4)

gl   bowl (K I.ii.18)

gl   R roll out (MR IV.33)

glgl   see *gl*

glḥ   G shave (A III.ii.32)

gly   N appear (B I.v.7)

gll   see *gl*

glṯ   snow (B Ia.7)

gm   also (B IV.viii.42)

gm   aloud (B II.iv.2)

gmd   G expand (?) (MR II. 14)

gml   sickle (MR V.42)

gmn   Gp be defiled (B VI.i. 19)

gmr   1. annihilator (B VI. vi.6)
       2. champion (B III.i. 46)
       3. fighting-cock (?) (B VI.vi.16)

gmr   G fulfil, accomplish (A III.iv.60)

gn   garden (B V.vi.21)

gngn   pipe, gullet (B IV.vii. 49)

gᶜr   G roar, rebuke (B III.i. 24)

gᶜt   lowing (K I.iii.18)

gp   shore (MR I.30)

gpn   1. vine (B III.i.43)
       2. rein (B IV.iv.5)

gpn w²ugr Gupanu-and-Ugaru (gods) (B I.iii.36)

gpr young hero (A III.i.11)

gpt slope (B IV.vii.36)

gr stranger, client (A III.iii.47)

gr R drag (MR I.66)

grgr throat (K III.i.48)

grgr see *gr*

grdš tumulus, ruin (K I.i.11)

gry G attack (K I.iii.6)

gry D appoint a deputy (B II.iv.12)

grn threshing-floor (A I.v.7)

gršʿ G chase away (B I.ii.15) N be chased (In III.9)

gšm rain-storm (MR IV.34)

gṯr Gathru (PN, spirit) (R III.11)

gṯrm du. of *gṯr*

d

d relat.pronoun (B I.iii.1)

d²iy pinion (A III.iii.2)

d²iy black kite (A II.iv.18)

d²it black kite (In V.8)

d²u black kite (In V.8)

d²y G 1. fly, float (A III.iii.9) 2. let fly (K III.v.47)

db²at head-dress (L II.ii.21)

dbb fly, winged monster, demon (B IV.i.39)

dbb see *ḏbb*

dbḥ G sacrifice (B II.iv.28) N be sacrificed (K II.iv.12)

dbḥ sacrifice, banquet (B IV.iii.17)

dbr steppe (B V.iii.12)

dbr D drive away (K III.vi.31)

dbr D speak (In I.8)

dg fish (MR I.63)

dgy fisherman (B I.vi.10)

dgl banner (A IVb.ii.3)

dgn 1. grain (K III.iii.13) 2. Daganu (god) (B II.iv.22)

dgt sea-animal (A III.iv.41)

dd love (B I.iii.5)

dd jar (B Ia.9)

dd N stand up (B I.i.8)

ddy mandrake (B I.iii.15)

ddn Didanu (PN, spirit) (R II.3); see *dtn*

dw sick (K III.ii.20)

dwd see *dd*

dwy   G be sick (K III.i.57)

dwṯ   see *dṯ*

dyn   see *dn*

dk   pure (B V.iii.8)

dkr   male (R III.19)

dkrt   bowl (B IV.vi.54)

dl   poor, weak (K III.vi.48)

dll   scout (B IV.vii.45)

dlp   G be unsteady (B III.iv. 17)

dlt   door (MR I.25)

dm   because, then (B V.iii. 9); see also *d*

dm   G mourn (K III.i.26)

dm   mourning   (MR II.ii. 47)

dm   1. blood (B I.ii.14)
        2. juice (MR III.31)
        3. coating (B IV.i.32)

dmgy   Damgayu (goddess) (MR II.i.16)

dmy   G remain quiet (K I. iii.10)

dmm   see *dm*

dmᶜ   G shed tears (A III.iv. 12)

dmᶜt   tear (A III.ii.33)

dmqt   Damiqtu (goddess) (MR V.50)

dmrn   1. destruction (B III. iii.13)

        2. Place of Perdition, Nether World (B IV. vii.39)

dn   G judge (B IV.iii.2)

dn   lawsuit (A I.v.8)

dn   D be very strong (K III. i.30)

dn   mighty (MR II.ii.58)

dn   vat (B I.i.12)

dnʾil   Daniʾilu (PN) (A I. i.6)

dnt   strife (B IV.iii.20)

dnty   Danatiya (PN) (A I.ii. 47)

dᶜ   bead of sweat (MR IV. 15)

dᶜṣ   D shuffle the feet (B I. v.4)

dᶜt   1. knowledge (B III.i. 16)

        2. acquaintance (B VI. vi.50)

dᶜt   pl. of *dᶜ*

dġt   D burn incense (MR I. 15)

dġt   incense (A III.iv.23)

dġtt   incense (MR I.15)

dq   small, delicate (B IV.i. 41)

dqn   chin (B V.vi.19)

dqn   old age (B I.v.2)

dqt small female cattle, ewe (R I.9)

dr generation, race, family (A III.iii.56)

drdr eternity (B III.iv.10)

dry G scatter, winnow (B VI.ii.32)

drk road (R III.6)

drk D tread (In I.37) Dp be treaded, loaded (bow) (A I.v.2)

drkt dominion (B I.iv.3)

dr^c G sow (B VI.ii.35)

drq Gt march, walk, approach (B I.iv.39)

dšn ointment (In V.5)

dt pl. of *d*

dt fem. of *d*

dtn Ditanu (PN, spirit) (K II.iii.4); see *ddn*

ḏt Gp be threshed (A II.i.19)

ḏtt fat ashes (R I.18)

ḏ

ḏbb Dhubabu (fly, winged monster) (B I.iii.46)

ḏbb see *dbb*

ḏd small herd (B IV.viii.54)

ḏd encampment (B I.v.7)

ḏd breast (MR I.59)

ḏhrt vision (K I.i.36)

ḏmr G protect (A I.i.28)

ḏmr protection (In. V.22)

ḏmr guard, soldier (B I.ii. 14)

ḏmr D play, make music (In V.3)

ḏnb tail (MR III.20)

dr^c 1. arm (B V.vi.20) 2. side (MR IV.8)

ḏrq red (B V.i.6)

ḏrt vision (K I.iii.47)

h

hbr G bow (B I.iii.9)

hg counting (K I.ii.38)

hd Haddu (god, = Ba^clu) (B Ia.1)

hdy G gash (B V.vi.19)

hdm stool (B I.ii.22)

hdr^cy Haddura^ciyu (city) (In V.3)

hdrt tremendous experience (K I.iii.51)

hw he (pers.pron.) (B III.i. 37)

hwy D crave (B IV.viii.50)

hwt him (pers.pron.) (B I. vi.20)

hwt word (B I.iii.14)

hy   she (pers.pron.) (A III. iv.39)

hyn   skilful (B I.vi.22)

hyt   her (pers.pron.) (B I. iii.10)

hk   powder (L II.i.2)

hkl   palace (B I.ii.18)

hl   look! (A I.v.12)

hlk   G go, flow (B I.iv.32)
Dt walk (B V.vi.26)
S make flow (B I.v.2)

hlk   1. course (A III.ii.3)
2. behaviour (In I.37)

hlk   behold! (A I.v.12)

hll   Hilalu (god) (A I.ii.27)

hlm   G strike (B III.i.5)

hlm   look! (B I.iii.32)

hln   look! (B I.ii.5)

hm   if, if only, when, or (B II.ii.24; iv.26; III.iv.2)

hm   G vibrate (A I.vi.12)

hm   they (pers.pron.) (A III. ii.35)

hm   confusion (In I.28)

hmlt   multitude (B I.iii.28)

hmm   see *hm*

hmry   Humurayu (city of Nether World (B IV.viii. 12)

hmt   them (pers.pron.) (B III.iv.36)

hn   look! (B VI.vi.48)

hn   hin-measure (MR I.75)

hndt   this (dem.pron.) (A III.iv.edge)

hpk   G 1. change into (B V. iii.12)
2. overturn (B III. iii.17)

hr   D fancy, covet (MR II.i. 39)

hr   conception (A I.i.40)

hrg   G kill (MR IV.5)

hrgb   Hargubu (bird) (A III. iii.15)

hry   G conceive (B V.vi.22)
S make conceive (MR II.i.6)

hrnmy   Harnamite (A I.i.18)

hrr   see *hr*

hrt   conception (A I.ii.41)

ht   now (B III.iv.8)

w

w   and, also, but (B I.iv.41)

why   see *yhy*

wld   see *yld*

wn   see *w*

wsr   see *ysr*

wpy   see *mšpy*

wpt   D spit (B IV.iii.13)

z

zbl G impregnate (MR IV.
   28)
zbl highness (B I.i.3)
zbl sick (K I.ii.45)
zbln illness (K I.i.17)
zbr G prune (MR I.9)
zd G 1. boil (MR V.8)
   2. covet (B II.v.13)
zd breast (MR I.24)
zwd see *zd*
znt maintenance (B II.iv.
   16)
zᶜtr see *ztr* (R III.3)
zġy G moo (K II.i.5)
zġt whining (K I.iii.18)
zr strange (In III.14)
zt olive (B V.ii.5)
ztr marjoram (A I.i.27)

ḥ

ḥbṭ G beat (In I.25)
ḥby steward (MR III.19)
ḥbl flock (B IV.vii.57)
ḥbl G truss up (In I.11)
ḥbl pain, pang (L II.ii.30)
ḥbq G hold, embrace (B III.
   i.41)
ḥbr companion, friend (In
   V.5)

ḥbš girdle, game-bag,
   carrying-net (B I.ii.13)
ḥgr G gird (K I.iii.44)
ḥdg litter (MR II.i.18)
ḥdy G watch, see (B I.ii.24)
   N be seen (B IV.vi.11)
ḥdr chamber (B I.v.11)
ḥdṯ G become new (A II.
   iv.9)
ḥdṯ new (K I.ii.49)
ḥdṯ new moon (R I.1)
ḥdṯ renewal, equinox (R I.
   48)
ḥwy G live (B I.v.30)
   D give life (A I.vi.31)
   Dp be given life (L II.
   ii.20)
ḥwy see *šhy*
ḥwr see *ḥr*
ḥwš see *ḥš*
ḥwt see *ḥt*
ḥwt region (B IV.i.42)
ḥṭb G gather wood (K I.
   iii.8)
ḥṭt wheat (K I.ii.29)
ḥz arrow (K I.iii.12)
ḥzr D make visit (B VI.v.
   23)
ḥzr residence (B I.iv.47)
ḥzt acumen, sharpness (B I.
   v.31)

ḥy   alive (B VI.iii.2)

ḥyl   host (A IVc.iii.12)

ḥym   life (B III.iv.2)

ḥkm   G be wise (B IV.iv.41)

ḥkm   wise (B I.v.30)

ḥkm   wisdom (B I.v.30)

ḥkmt   wisdom (B IV.v.4)

ḥkpt   Egypt (B I.vi.13)

ḥkr   distress (In IV.6)

ḥl   1. strength, force
         (MR III. 27)

       2. bastion (K III.i.7)

       3. host (R I.47)

ḥl   D purify (R IV.23)

ḥlb   milk (MR I.14)

ḥly   D beseech (A III.ii.15)

ḥlm   dream (B VI.iii.4)

ḥln   window (B IV.v.62)

ḥlq   buttock (?) (B I.ii.14)

ḥm   heat (B III.iv.33)

ḥmd   G crave, covet (B Ia.8)

ḥmdrt   shriveled stalks
         (A III.ii.21)

ḥmḥm   passion (K III.i.29)

ḥmḥmt   heat, orgasm (A I.i.
         40)

ḥmyt   wall (R IV.27)

ḥmk   young deer (B II.v.5)

ḥmṣ   G 1. (turn sour)

       2. be parched (A
         III.i.17)

ḥmr   ass (K I.iii.17)

ḥmr   clay (B IV.viii.56)

ḥmt   wine-skin (K III.iii.15)

ḥmt   wall (K I.ii.22)

ḥmt   poison (In I.32)

ḥmṯ   abdomen (In I.7)

ḥn   D show favour (L II.i.
         12)

ḥnt   mercy (A I.i.16)

ḥsn   grasshopper (K I.iii.1)

ḥsp   G scoop up (A III.ii.2)

ḥp   G rustle (A IVc.iii.12)

ḥpn   1. (fist)

       2. prime strength
         (B III.i.9)

ḥpp   see *ḥp*

ḥpš   G pick straw (K I.iii.8)

ḥṣ   gravel (B II.iv.11)

ḥr   G become hot (MR II.
         ii.37)

       D scorch, roast (B V.
         ii.5)

ḥr   G go back (In I.13)

ḥrb   1. knife (B I.i.7)

       2. sword (B III.iv.4)

ḥrḥrt   fever (B III.iii.13)

ḥry   Hariya (PN) (K I.iii.
         39)

ḥryt   Hryt (city) (MR VI.36)

ḥrn   Horonu (god) (B III.
         i.7)

ḫrn Horonite, demon (In I.27)

ḫrnq flower-garden (MR V. 23)

ḫrṣ rotting (A III.i.10)

ḫrṣ potash (A I.vi.37)

ḫrr see _ḫr_

ḫrš Gt perform magic (K III.v.26)

ḫrš magic, spell (B II.ii.4)

ḫrš artisan (B I.vi.23)

ḫrṯ G plough (B V.vi.20)

_ḫš_ G hurry (B I.iii.18)

ḫšn bliss (B V.iii.3)

_ḫt_ G circle round (B IV.vii. 58)

ḫtk G have authority (B VI. vi.46)

ḫtk authority, patronage (K I.i.10; In V.23)

ḫtk sire, father (K III.ii.12)

ḫtk child (L II.iii.34)

ḫtl swaddling-clothes (MR II.i.19)

ḫtp type of sacrifice (R IV. 32)

ḫtt disease (In I.23)

ḫtṯ silver (K I.ii.18)

_ḫṯ_ unseasoned bread (R I. 22)

ḫ

ḫbl mess (B II.iv.8)

ḫbr Khuburu (city) (K I.i.2)

ḫbrṯ washing-copper (B IV. ii.9)

_ḫd_ thunderstorm (MR IV. 34)

ḫdd thunderstorm (K I.ii. 39)

ḫwl see _ḫl_

_ḫḫ_ filth, slime (B IV.viii. 13)

_ḫt_ G awake (K I.iii.50)

_ḫt_ stick (A III.i.14)

ḫtʾ G miss, sin (In III.5) S cause to miss (A III. iii.45)

ḫyt see _ḫt_

ḫyl see _ḫl_

ḫym baldachin (B IV.i.29)

ḫyr see _ḫr_

_ḫl_ G convulse (L II.ii.29) L make convulse (MR V.5)

ḫlb forested hill (B V.v.14)

ḫlln pangs, childbirth (A I. ii.42)

ḫlpn dagger (A III.iv.44)

ḫlṣ purified milk (In III.7)

ḫlq G disappear, perish (B V.vi.10)

ḫm tent (K II.iv.23)

ḫmʾat butter (MR I.14)

ḫmr foaming wine (B I.i.16)

ḫmš D do for the fifth time (K III.v.17)

ḫmš fifth (B IV.vi.29)

ḫmšt one fifth (shekel) (K I.i.30)

ḫmt shed (canvas) (K I.ii.12)

ḫnzr boar, metaph. meteorological or astronomical phenomenon (B V.v.9)

ḫnp D treat viciously (In I.15)
N be defiled (K III.iv.14)

ḫnp viciousness (A I.vi.42)

ḫs G be sharp, remember (K II.iii.25)
D stimulate (B IV.iv.39)

ḫss see ḫs and kṯr

ḫsp G droop (A III.i.31)

ḫsr G lack (B VI.ii.17)

ḫp shore (B I.ii.7)

ḫpy G break (In I.6)

ḫprt ewe (B IV.vi.48)

ḫptr cauldron (B IV.ii.8)

ḫpṯ release, weaning of cattle (K II.i.6)

ḫpṯ free man, conscript (K I.ii.37)

ḫpṯt freedom (B V.v.15)

ḫṣb Gt/Dt slaughter (B I.ii.6)

ḫr free man (B III.i.41)

ḫr Khurri (Hurri, country) (R III.1)

ḫr G be excellent (MR IV.17)

ḫrʾu faeces (MR III.21)

ḫrb G dry up (A III.i.30)

ḫrḫb Khirikhbi (god) (MR V.2)

ḫrṭ G pluck (MR I.38)

ḫrẓ^c toe (?) (MR II.i.41)

ḫry Khurrian (Hurrian) (R III.22)

ḫrm D destroy under the ban (MR IV.3)

ḫrn caravan (B IV.v.13)

ḫrp (autumnal) mental disturbance, insanity (In I.18)

ḫrpn autumnal (MR III.31)

ḫrṣ gold (B I.iii.47)

ḫršn Khurshanu (mountain) (B II.ii.3)

ḫrt grave (B V.v.5)

ḫš G invade (B IV.vii.32)

ḫš silent, unconscious (MR III.29)

ḫšy   see _ḫš_

ḫšš   see _ḫš_

ḫšt   basement (K III.i.3)

_ḫt_   G 1. be shattered
(K III.vi.1)
2. be terrified (In II.
12)
Dp become weak (B III.
iv.1)

ḫtˀ   N disappear (B IV.viii.
20)

ḫtn   G betroth (MR V.32)

ḫtn   son-in-law (MR V.25)

ḫtt   see _ḫt_

ḫtr   sieve (B VI.ii.32)

ṭ

_ṭb_   good, sweet (B I.i.20)

_ṭb_   G be good (MR IV.21)

ṭbḫ   G slaughter (B II.iv.30)

ṭbn   delight (A III.i.46)

ṭbq   G put the lid on (A I.i.
28)

ṭhr   pure (B IV.v.19)

ṭhr   see _ẓhr_

ṭwb   see _ṭb_

ṭwḫ   see _ṭḫ_

ṭḥn   G grind (B VI.ii.34)

_ṭḫ_   G plaster (A I.i.32)

_ṭṭ_   see _ṭṭ_ and _ẓẓ_

_ṭl_   dew (B I.ii.39)

_ṭl_   D let fall dew (A III.i.41)

ṭlb   G seek (B V.iv.2)

ṭly   Tallayu (goddess)
(B Ia.5)

ṭll   see _ṭl_

ṭmṭ   G menstruate (In I.7)

ṭˁn   G pierce (B IV.viii.68)

ṭrd   G expel (B I.iii.47)

ṭry   fresh (B VI.vi.43)

_ṭṭ_   mud (B II.iv.8)

ẓ

ẓˀu   origin. habitat (B I.iii.
2)

_ẓb_   see _ṭb_

ẓby   (1. gazelle)
2. metaph. leader
(K II.iv.7)

ẓhr   pure (MR V.21)

ẓhr   see _ṭhr_

ẓwm   see _ẓm_

ẓḥq   G laugh (MR II.i.12)

ẓḥq   see _ṣḥq_

_ẓẓ_   1. mud (In I.42)
2. Zizzu (god) (MR VI.
36)

_ẓẓ_   see _ṭṭ_

_ẓl_   1. shadow (B I.v.12)
2. sheen, glitter (B IV.ii.
26)

ẓlm   deep darkness (In III.8)

ẓlmt   deep darkness (B IV. vii.55)

ẓm   G fast (In III.7)

ẓm^ʾ   D be thirsty (K II.i.2)

ẓm^ʾ   see *ġm^ʾ*

ẓn   suspect(?) (In I.20)

ẓr   back, top (B I.iii.3a)

ẓš   fluttering (L II.iii.15)

y

y   O! (B I.v.20)

y   woe! (A III.iii.46)

yb   G yell (A III.iii.40)

ybb   see *yb*

ybl   G carry, bring (B I.v. 34)

　　　Gp be brought (A III. iv.50)

　　　S let bring (B Ia.10)

ybl   yield (B V.ii.5)

ybl   urge, wish (A III.iv.61)

ybl   support (B IV.i.37)

yblt   outgrowth, wart (MR VI.66)

ybm   G fulfil the nuptial duty (B VI.i.31)

　　　St proclaim oneself a widow to be married (B VI.i.30)

ybm   orphan-brother (K III. ii.32)

ybmt   widow to be married by the next of kin of her husband; 'wanton' widow (B I.ii.33)

ybnt   see *ybmt*

ybrdmy   Yabridamayu (goddess) (MR V.29)

ygrš   Yagrush (name of weapon) (B III.i.5)

yd   1. hand (B I.i.11)
　　　2. metaph. penis (MR I. 33)

yd   with (A I.i.3)

yd   affection (B I.iii.6)

ydd   beloved (B V.i.8)

ydy   G 1. cast out, expel, remove (B VI. vi.52)

　　　2. place, found (MR I.4)

　　　3. praise (A III.iv. 25)

　　　Gp be removed (B IV. vi.33)

ydy   G scratch (B V.vi.18)

ydn   D beat, whip (A III.ii. 12)

yd^c   G know (B I.i.25)

*yd*ᶜ   G sweat (B I.iii.34)

ydt   portion (B IV.viii.59)

yh   Ha! (B II.iii.7)

yw   Yawwu (god) (B II.iv. 12)

yhd   single man (K I.ii.43)

yhy   G rush along (MR II. i.35)

Dt hasten (B I.iii.20)

yhmr   roebuck (B VI.i.28)

yhr   lizard (MR VI.73)

ytp   Yattupa (god) (A II. iv.7) = *ytpn*

ytpn   Yattupanu (god) (A II. iv.6)

*yẓ*ʾ   G go out (MR II.i.14)

*yẓ*ʾ   see *yṣ*ʾ

yl   G wail (K III.ii.28)

yld   G bear (MR II.i.27)

Gp be born (A I.ii.14)

D make bear, beget (MR I.53)

S beget (B V.ii.24)

yld   child (B III.iii.14)

yly   friend (MR II.ii.51)

yll   see *yl*

ylt   see *yld*

ym   1. sea (B I.ii.7)

2. Yammu (god) (B I. iii.39)

ym   day (B II.ii.12)

*ym*ʾ*an*   Yamʾanu (country) (B IV.i.42)

ymmt   see *ybmt*

ymn   right (hand) (B I.v.22)

ymn   L aim with the right hand (MR I.37)

yn   wine (B Ia.9)

ynq   G imbibe, suck (MR I.24)

S suckle (K II.ii.28)

ynt   pigeon (R I.10)

ysd   G found, establish (B IV.iii.6)

ysm   delight (L II.ii.30)

ysm   R be delicious (L I.3)

ysmsm(t)   1. delight (A I.ii. 42)

2. most comforta- ble part (A III. ii.11)

ysmt   delightfulness (name of Nether World) (B V. vi.7)

ysr   G instruct   (B IV.v.4)

Dt instruct (K III.vi.26)

*y*ᶜ*bdr*   ample flowing (na- me?) (B I.iv.52)

*y*ᶜ*l*   mountain-goat (B VI.i. 26)

*y*ᶜ*r*   forest (B IV.vii.36)

*y*ᶜ*r*   razor (B V.vi.18)

yġl lean stalk (A III.ii.14)

yp beautiful (L II.iii.3)

ypy R beautify oneself (B I.iii.1)

yp^c G rise, appear (B I.iii.37)

  N appear (B V.iv.8)

ypp see *ypy*

yṣ^ʾ G 1. go out (B II.ii.9)

  2. pass (time) (A I.ii.44)

  3. appear (messenger) (A III.ii.28)

  S make go out (B III.iv.2)

yṣb G load (bow) (A I.vi.13)

  Gp be loaded (A I.vi.9)

yṣb Yassubu (PN) (K II.ii.25)

yṣq G pour, smelt (B IV.i.25)

  Gp be poured (B I.ii.31)

yṣr G form (In III.17)

  Gp be formed (K III.v.30)

yqẓ G awake (A III.iii.40)

yqy G protect (B III.i.18)

yqġ G pay attention (K III.vi.30)

yqr costly (B II.iii.8)

yqr Yaqaru (PN, spirit) (In V.2)

yr rainshower (K I.ii.40)

yr^ʾ G fear (B V.ii.6)

yrgb Yaraggib (god or spirit) (B VI.vi.58)

yrd G descend (B III.iii.20)

  S make descend (K I.ii.24)

yrḫ 1. moon (B V.iii.7)

  2. Yarikhu (god) (MR V.4)

yrḫ month (B II.v.3)

yry G throw, shoot (A III.i.40)

yrk (1. thigh)

  2. spur of mountain (L II.iii.27)

yrkt winglet, fruit of ash-tree (MR IV.14)

yrq (1. yellow)

  2. gold (B IV.iv.6)

yrt Yarti (city) (MR I.75)

yrṯ G inherit (B III.i.19)

  Gt take possession (B I.iii.47)

yšn G fall asleep (K I.i.31)

yšr fairness (K I.i.13)

ytm orphan (A I.v.8)

ytmt orphan (In I.22)

ytn G 1. give, place (B I.i. 10)

2. give (voice) (In I. 37)

3. allow (K II.ii.10)

Gp 1. be given (B IV.v. 27)

2. be allowed (K II. ii.10)

N be given (voice) (K III.i.4)

ytnt gift (K I.iii.31)

yṯb G sit, dwell (B Ia.1)

S make sit, dwell (B IV.v.47)

yṯᶜ G save, deliver (A II.i. 12)

yṯq G bind (MR VI.6)

k

k 1. like, as (B Ia.1)

2. surely (B Ia.9)

k 1. surely (A I.v.ii)

2. when, although (B V. i.7)

3. because (MR IV.24)

4. that (B I.v.28)

kbd 1. liver, middle (B I.ii. 25)

2. bosom (MR II.i.9)

kbd D honour (B I.vi.20)

kbd honour (K I.v.24)

kbd heavy, full (R I.39)

kbkb star (B I.ii.41)

kbkbt female star (MR IV. 17)

kbrt riddle (B VI.v.16)

kd 1. when (B IV.iii.12)

2. because (B I.iv.23)

3. in case (B I.v.3)

4. thus (A III.i.14)

kd pitcher, jug (B I.i.6)

kdd child (A I.vi.52)

kdrt clod, lump (B I.ii.9)

khn priest (B VI.vi.56)

kwn see *kn*

kḥṯ throne (B I.iv.3)

kkb star (L II.i.4)

kknt bucket or narrow jar (B VI.i.67)

kl D complete (B IV.v. 10)

kl totality, all (B I.v.33)

kl equipment (A I.vi.40)

klʾ G/D close (B I.ii.3)

klʾat pair, both (B I.i.11)

klb dog (A III.i.13)

klbt bitch (B I.iii.45)

kly G cease, be spent (K III.iii.13)

D complete, finish,

consume, destroy
(B I.iii.39)
(B VI.vi.10)
(N be completed)

klyt   kidney (In I.3)

kll   see *kl*

klt   bride (B I.i.26)

klt   totality (K I.ii.16)

km   see *k*

kmm   ditto (R I.29)

kmn   surface measure (B I.
iv.38)

kms   Gt knuckle down
(MR II.ii.54)

kmṯ   Kamathu (god)
(MR VI.36)

kn   G be, be reliable
(K I.i.15)
(A I.i.25)
L create (B I.v.36)
S create (K III.v.26)

kn   thus (MR II.ii.53)

kn   reliable, enduring
(MR I.54)

kny   Gp be respectable (B I.
i.27)

knkn   pipe, tunnel (B V.v.
13)

knp   wing (A III.iii.1)

knr   lyre (B I.iii.4)

knrt   Kinnereth (city) (A III.
iii.41)

ks   cup (B I.i.10)

ksʾan   birth-stool (MR II.i.
18)

ksʾu   chair (B I.ii.21)

ksy   G cover oneself (B V.vi.
16)
D cover (L II.iii.24)

ksl   1. spine (B I.iii.33)
2. stave of bow (B I.ii.
16)

ksm   emmer-corn (B V.vi.5)

ksp   silver (B I.iii.46)

kst   covering, garment
(A III.i.36)

kp   1. palm, hand (B I.ii.10)
2. tray (MR V.35)

kpr   henna (B I.ii.2)

kpt   palm-frond (In I.17)

kptr   Kaphtor (Crete) (B I.
vi.14)

kpṯ   royal cap (In V.8)

kr   ram (B IV.vi.47)

kr   R drum (B IV.iv.29)

krb   G be distressed (A III.
i.2)

kry   G dig (MR II.i.23)

krkr   see *kr*

krm   vineyard (A III.i.31)

kr^c G kneel (L II.ii.18)

krpn beaker (B I.i.11)

krt Kirtu (PN) (K I.i.1)

krtn Kirtanu = Kirtu
(K III.i.39)

kš gourd (A IVc.iv.15)

kš see *kt̲*

kšd G attract (B IV.viii.53)

kšp sorcerer (In III.9)

kšp sorcery (B II.ii.5)

kt socle (B IV.i.30)

ktms knuckling under
(B VI.i.52)

ktn chemise (R III.4)

ktp 1. shoulder(-blade)
(B III.i.5)
(MR III.11)
2. axe-head (B VI.v.2)

kt̲ gourd, bowl (B Ia.8)

kt̲ see *kš*

kt̲r D exploit well (B IV.ii.
30)

kt̲r (1. success)
2. childbirth (K I.i.16)

kt̲r skilled person (B III.iii.
20)

kt̲r wḫss Kotharu-and-Kha-
sisu (god) (B I.vi.21)

kt̲rt Kathiratu (goddesses)
(A I.ii.26)

l

l to, for, on, from, about
(B Ia.3; I.ii.12; A III.i.1)

l 1. not (B I.i.14)
2. surely (B I.iv.37)

l O! (B I.vi.10)

lʾ G be soiled (B I.v.18)

lʾan power (In V.22)

lʾim people, nation (B I.
ii.7)

lʾy G 1. be strong (K III.
vi.2)
2. overpower (K I.i.
33)
N be overpowered, be-
come weak (MR VI.
68)

lʾy see *lʾ*

lʾk G send (B III.i.11)
N be sent (B IV.v.42)

lb 1. heart (B I.ii.26)
2. pith (MR III.29)

lbʾu lion (B IV.viii.49)

lbd alone (B III.iii.20)

lbn white (B V.iii.6)

lbn G make bricks (B IV.
iv.61)

lbnn Lebanon (mountain)
(A I.vi.21)

lbnt   brick (B IV.iv.62)

lbš   G put on clothes (A III.
iv.44)

      Gp be covered (MR IV.
25)

      S clothe (B V.v.3)

lbš   garment (In III.12)

lbšt   garment (K III.ii.29)

lg   log-measure (MR I.75)

lwy   S encircle (K I.iii.45)

lwn   follower (B III.i.46)

lḥ   G 1. provide with beve-
rage (K II.iv.12)

      2. moisten (B V.ii.21)

lḥ   tablet (B III.i.26)

lḥ   cheek (B V.vi.19)

lḥḥ   see *lḥ*

lḥk   D lick (In II.5)

lḥm   G eat (B IV.vi.55)

      D give to eat (A I.i.2)

      S give to eat (B I.i.5)

lḥm   grain, bread (K III.iii.
14; A I.vi.2)

lḥt   abuse, slander (A I.i.28)

lḥš   D charm (MR VI.5)

lḥšt   whisper (B I.iii.23)

lṭpn   benevolent (Ilu) (B II.
iii.21)

lṭš   G sharpen (B III.i.32)

lẓt   mockery, scoffing (In
III.11)

lyn   see *ln*

lyt   wreath (B Ia.10; B VI.
iv.19)

lkt   see *hlk*

ll   (1. night)

      2. Lelu (mountain or
god) (B III.i.14)

ll   night-demon (In I.15)

llʾu   lambkin (B II.iv.32)

llt   night (K III.i.32)

lm   1. why ? (B III.i.24)

      2. why not ? (L II.iii.5)

lm   see *l*

lmd   D teach (A II.i.29)

lmd   pupil, student (B VI.vi.
55)

ln   G spend the night (A I.
i.5)

lsm   G run (B I.iii.19)

lsm   sporting-dog (?) (B VI.
vi.21)

lsmt   haste (A IVc.iv.6)

lpš   clothing (B V.vi.16)

lṣb   frown (B IV.iv.28)

lqḥ   G take (B I.i.16)

lrgt   Larugat (city) (MR VI.
26)

lrmn   pomegranate (MR I.
50)

lšn   tongue (B V.ii.3)

lšn   D scold, denounce
(A I.vi.51)

lty   twig (A IVb.i.9)

ltn   Lotanu (Leviathan, monster) (B V.i.1)

lṯ   Gp be moulded (K III. v.38; In III.17)

m

m   what ? (K I.i.38)

m'ad   numerous (K I.ii.35)

m'at   hundred (K I.ii.36)

m'id   much, very(ly) (B I.ii. 23)

m'izrtm   du. loin-cloth (B V. vi.17)

m'iyt   lowland (K III.iii.4)

m'iyt   see *mhyt*

m'inš   meeting-place (A III. iv.48)

m'it   hundred (B V.iv.3)

m'ud   much (B V.iii.16)

m'd   D multiply (K I.ii.5)

mbk   fountain-head (B I.v.6)

mgdl   tower (A II.i.31)

mgn   G give presents (B IV. iii.25)

mgn   present (B IV.i.21)

mgṯ   selected, choice lamb (K III.vi.18)

md   G measure off (A I.ii. 41)

md   clothing (B IV.ii.6)

mdb   ocean, Flood (B Ia.2)

mdb   monster inhabiting the ocean (In I.27)

mdbḥ   altar (R I.41)

mdbḥt   altar (MR IV.16)

mdbr   desert (MR II.i.21)

mdgt   mausoleum (A III.iii. 41)

mdd   beloved (B I.iii.38)

mdd   see *md*

mdw   illness (K III.vi.35)

mdl   (thunder)bolt (B I.iv. 26)

mdl   D saddle (cloth only) (B IV.iv.4)

mdnt   coll. veterans (?) (B I.ii.16)

*md*ᶜ   friend (K II.iv.13)

*mdr*ᶜ   sown land (MR I.69)

mdt   see *md*

mḏr   vow (R IV.30)

mh   what? (B I.v.28)

mh   water (B I.ii.38)

mhyt   watered land, lowland (B V.vi.5); see *m'iyt*

mhmrt   gullet, libation-pipe (B V.i.7)

mhr   agile warrior (B I.ii.11)

mhr   bridal gift, bridal price (MR VI.73)

mwt   see *mt*

mzl G donate generously (K I.ii.46)

mzn food, victuals (R III.5)

mznm du. scales, balance (MR V.34)

*mz*ᶜ Dp be rent (A III.i.36)

mḥy G wipe (R I.54)
  N be wiped (B I.ii.30)
  S make wipe (B V.ii.25)

mḥmd choice, best (B IV.v.16)

mḥrtt plough-land (B VI.iv.3)

mḫ marrow (K III.i.27)

mḫ marrow-like, smoothly (A I.i.38)

mḫy G remove (K III.v.30)

mḫlpt pl. tresses (A III.ii.33)

mḫnm Makhanami (city) (In II.4)

mḫṣ G strike (B I.ii.7)
  Gt fight (B I.ii.5)

mḫr G rival (L I.7)

mḫš G slay (B I.iii.38)

mṭ staff (B I.ii.15)

mṭ below (B III.i.9)

mṭnt plastered cup (In I.34)

mṭᶜt plantation (A IVb.ii.7)

mṭr G rain (B VI.iii.6)

mṭr rain (K III.iii.5)

mṭt bed (K I.i.30)

*mz*ʾ G find (MR II.i.37)

mẓll shelter (B I.iv.48)

my what about? (B V.vi.23)

my who? (K III.v.10)

my water (A III.ii.1)

mk G go down (B III.iv.17)

mk pit (B IV.viii.12)

mk then (B IV.vi.31)

mkk see *mk*

mknpt crest (K III.i.9)

mknt dwelling-place (K I.i.11)

mks covering (B IV.ii.5)

ml D rub (B Ia.6)

*ml*ʾ G be filled, full (B I.ii.25)
  D fill (B V.iv.17)

*ml*ʾ*ak* 1. messenger (B III.i.11)
  2. angel (MR IV.25)

*ml*ʾ*u* full (L II.iii.8)

mlghy Mulugu-hiya (goddess) (MR V.47)

mlḥ Gp be salted (B I.i.7)

mlḥm war (B V.ii.23)

mlḥmt war (B I.iii.15)

mlḥmt bread (?) (alt. in B I.iii.15)

mlk   G be king (B IV.iii.9)
D make king (B
VI.i.46)

mlk   king (B I.v.8)

mlk   kingship (B I.iv.2)

mlk   counselor (MR V.2)

mlk   Maliku (god) (MR VI.
41)

mlkt   queen (MR I.7)

mlkt   kingship (R IV.25)

mll   crumbs (B II.iv.11)

mll   see *ml*

mm   water (K III.i.34)

mmᶜ   gore, bowels (B I.ii.
14)

mmt   place of death (B III.
i.9)

mn   what? (B I.iii.37)

mn   who? (B V.iv.23)

mn   how many? (K III.ii.19)

mn   incantation (A III.i.11)

mn   caterpillar (B III.iv.3)

mndᶜ   perhaps (K III.ii.24)

mnḥy   tribute (B III.i.38)

mnḫ   resting-place (B III.
iv.3)

mnm   whatever (B I.iv.4)

mnt   1. limb (B VI.ii.36)
2. portion (A I.i.32)
3. Fate (B IV.vii.56)

mnt   1. enumeration
(MR V.46)
2. incantation (K III.
v.45)

msdt   foundation (B IV.i.40)

mswn   night-quarters (K I.
iii.21)

msk   G mix (B I.i.17)

msk   mixture (B I.i.17)

msk   screen of door (In I.21)

mslmt   stairs (L II.iii.28)

mspr   recitation (B IV.v.42)

msrr   see *sr*

mᶜ   emphasizing particle
(B III.iii.15)

mᶜbd   place of worship
(MR IV.16)

mᶜd   congregation (B III.i.
14)

mᶜk   crumbs (K III.iv.5)

mᶜll   work, task (A III.ii.36;
MR V.43f.)

mᶜlt   steps, staircase (R I.
23)

mᶜmᶜ   intestinal trouble (In
I.41)

mᶜrb   sunset (A III.iv.48)

mᶜrb   temple rate (R I.19)

mġd   provisions (K I.ii.31)

mġz   bribe (B IV.i.23)

mġy G arrive (B I.ii.17)

mpḫm du. bellows (B IV.i. 23)

mpr heart (A II.iv.26)

mṣ G suck (K II.ii.27)

mṣb standard (MR V.34)

mṣbṭ handle-bar (B IV.i.24)

mṣd banquet (K I.ii.26)

mṣd fortress (MR VI.57)

mṣḫ G pull down (B I.v.1)

mṣlt libation-vat (MR II.ii. 61)

mṣltm du. cymbals (A III. iv.26)

mṣṣ see *mṣ*

mṣr stronghold (B I.v.8)

mṣrp crucible (In I.33)

mṣt dregs (MR II.ii.28)

mqm place (K I.i.47)

mqr well (K I.v.2)

mr G (1. be bitter)
2. make strong, forti-
fy (A I.i.24)
3. expel (B III.iv.19)
N be fortified (A III.iv. 33)

mr bitter (A III.i.6)

mr 1. bitterness (K II.iv. 23)
2. pain (MR II.i.11)

mr myrrh (R I.20)

mr Mari (city) (MR VI. 34b)

mrʾ G fatten (B IV.vii.50)
N be fattened (B IV. viii.45)

mrʾu fatling (B I.i.8)

mrg S rub, polish (B IV.i. 32)

mrzḥ religious drinking so-
ciety (B II.iv.4)

mrzᶜ see *mrzḥ*

mrḥ nostrils (K III.i.47)

mrḥ lance (B VI.i.51)

mrym height (B II.iv.1)

mrkbt chariot (K I.i.49)

mrmt height (In III.7)

mrġt wife, lover (MR IV. 24)

mrġt see *rġt*

mrṣ G be ill (K III.i.56)

mrṣ ill (K III.ii.19)

mrṣ illness (K III.v.15)

mrr see *mr*

mrrt (1. gall-bladder)
2. Mirartu (city) (A III.iii.51)

mrṯ must (A IVc.iv.18)

mšdpt see *ndp*

mšḥ G anoint (L II.ii.23)

mšḫṭ slaughtering-axe (B III.i.39)

mškb bed (K III.ii.51)

mškn dwelling (K II.iii.19)

mšknt dwelling (A I.v.32)

mšlt rulership (B III.i.5)

mšmš marsh (MR II.ii.36)

mšnqt see *ynq*

mšpy announcer (K III.iv.14)

mšr S cleave (B I.vi.9)

mšrr counter-weight (MR V.36)

mšt banquet (In V.9)

mštᶜlt see *ᶜly*

mt G die (B II.ii.8)

mt 1. death (A III.i.17)
2. Motu (god) (B I.v.18)

mt dead (B V.vi.9)

mt man, husband (B I.i.13)

mtḥ (1. donkey-pack)
2. stratum, layer (B I.iv.36)

mtk libation (R IV.25)

mtn string, tendon (A I.vi.12)

mtn G wait (K III.i.36)

mtn gift (B II.v.12)

mtnm du. loins (MR II.ii.38)

mtnt grain-offering (R I.21)

mtᶜ G carry off (B IV.ii.6)

mtq sweet (MR I.50)

mtr S cut off (R I.2)

mtrḫt see *trḫ*

mtt gift (L II.i.13)

mtt state of death (B III.iv.1)

mṯ twin-brother (B V.v.22)

mṯb dwelling (K II.iv.22)

mṯbt dwelling (MR I.19)

mṯk G draw (K II.i.1)

mṯn repetition, another matter (B I.iv.31)

mṯpd (1. donkey-pack)
2. layer (B I.iv.35)

mṯpṭ judgeship (B III.iii.18)

mṯt lady (A I.v.16)

n

nʾṣ G revile (B II.iv.23)

nb abundant rain (B I.iii.3b)

nb G overgrow, cover (B IV.i.31)

nbṭ Gt be seen (B IV.iii.21)

nbk fountain (R I.32)

nblʾat flame (B IV.vi.23)

nbᶜ G rise (In II.10)

nbt honey (B VI.iii.7)

ngb   N be provisioned (K I.ii.32)

ngḥ   N gore each other (B VI.vi.17)

ngy   G go away (K I.iii.27)

ngr   (1. raven)
2. herald (K III.iv.3)

ngrt   (1. female raven)
2. heraldess (K III. iv.4)

ngš   G approach (B VI.ii. 21)
D bring near (MR III. 19)

ngṯ   G scrutinize (B II.v.4)
D seek (B VI.ii.6)

nd   G 1. fly away (A IVa. ii.4)
2. flee (A II.i.26)
D cause to fly, chase (A IVc.iv.10)

nd   trembling (L II.iii.16)

ndd   see *dd*

ndd   see *nd*

ndp   S throw (K I.iii.14)

ndr   G vow (K I.iv.37)

ndr   vow (K II.iii.26)

nhmmt   slumber (K I.i.32)

nhqt   braying (K I.iii.17)

nhr   (1. river)
2. Naharu (= Yammu, god) (B I.iii.39)

nwb   see *nb*

nwd   see *nd*

nwḫ   see *nḫ*

nws   see *ns*

nwt   habitation (B II.iii.8)

nzl   presentation (K I.ii. 16)

nḥy   G lean, droop (A III.i. 18)

nḥy   G bring tribute (K II. i.7)

nḥlt   heritage (B I.iii.30)

nḥn   we (pers.pron.) (MR II.i.5)

nḥš   serpent (MR VI.4)

nḥt   D lower (B III.iv.10)

nḫ   G rest (B VI.iii.18)

nḫl   wadi, brook (B VI.iii.7)

nḫnpt   see *ḫnp*

nḫt   seat, cushion (B I.iv.3)

nṭ   G leap, shake (B I.iii.33)
D leap, assail (In I.9)

nṭṭ   see *nṭ*

nṭm   G arrange, lay (In I.7)

nẓp   G drip (MR IV.15)

nyr   lamp (K III.i.37)

nky   G strike, pound (K III. ii.27)

nkl   Nikkalu (goddess) (MR V.1)

nkr   G leave (MR VI.62)

nkr   stranger (K I.ii.49)

nmrt beneficial strength (In V.23)

nn fish (B V.ii.27)

ns G flee (B IV.iii.5)

nsy G remove (MR VI.66)

nsy Gt be tested (B III.iv.4)

nsk G pour (B I.ii.40)
S make pour (MR IV.6)

nskt shower (B I.iii.3b.)

*ns*ᶜ G pull out (B III.iii.17)

*n*ᶜ*l* couch (B IV.i.36)

*n*ᶜ*m* 1. good, happy (K III. v.29)
2. gracious, lovely (B I.i.19)

*n*ᶜ*m* grace, loveliness (K I. iii.41)

*n*ᶜ*my* happiness (name of the Nether World) (B V.iii.3)

*n*ᶜ*my* Nuᶜmayu (PN) (K I. v.15)

*n*ᶜ*mn* gracious (B I.iii.3b)

*n*ᶜ*mt* grace (MR I.28)

*n*ᶜ*r* boy, lad (K I.ii.5)

*n*ᶜ*r* D shake out (MR VI. 65)

nġṣ G shake, quiver (B I.iii. 34)

nġr G watch, guard (MR I. 68)

N watch oneself (B IV. viii.14)

nġš G incline (L II.i.8)

np Noph (Memphis, city) (B I.vi.9)

npd G eat, devour (B V.i.5)

npyn skirt (B IV.ii.5)

npk spring (K I.iii.9)

npl G fall (B III.i.9)
Gt fall (K I.i.21)
N have fallen (B V. vi.8)

npṣ equipment, gear (A I. i.33)

npr fowl (B VI.ii.37)

npr see *pr*

npš 1. throat (B IV.vii.48)
2. soul (B II.ii.9)
3. living being (B IV. viii.50)
4. appetite (B IV.viii. 49)

npš G expand (heart) (In IV.5)

npšn underwear (B III.iii. 20)

nṣ S make fly up (B I.iv.1)

nṣb G 1. erect, set up (A I.i. 26)
2. direct, turn (K III.i.52)

nṣḥy   victory (A III.ii.36)

nṣṣ   see *nṣ*

nṣr   G shriek (K III.ii.25)

nqb   G name (A I.v.35)

nqbn   strap (B IV.iv.6)

nqd   breeder of small cattle, spiritual leader (B VI.vi.56)

nqh   G recover (In III.5)

nqmd   Niqmaddu (PN, spirit) (R II.12)

nqp   G turn round (In I.23)

nqpnt   cycle (MR II.ii.45)

nqpt   cycle (MR I.67)

nr   fire, blaze (A III.iii.52)

nr   musician (A III.i.8)

nrd   nard (?) (B I.ii.1)

nrt   lamp (B I.v.17)

nrt   sheen (B IV.ii.27)

nrt   tilth (K III.iii.10)

nšʾ   G 1. lift up, carry (B I.iii.35)
2. arise (MR I.54)
Gt arise (A I.v.6)
N be carried (B. II.ii.6)

nšb   haunch (B II.v.6)

nšg   plaited bag (A III.iv.45)

nšy   N be forgotten (B IV.viii.67)
S allow to forget (In I.5)

nšm   pl. people, men (B I.iii.27)

nšq   G kiss (B III.iv.4)

nšr   eagle (B III.iv.13)

ntb   path (A I.vi.43)

ntbt   path (R IV.33)

ntk   G pour out (A III.ii.33)
Gt be poured out (MR II.ii.56)
D pour out (K I.i.28)
S make pour out (MR II.ii.59)
St be induced to pour out (MR II.ii.57)

ntn   see *ytn*

ntr   G 1. jump, set off, start (B I.v.5; A I.vi.46)
2. make jump (B VI.vi.53)
S cause to fly up (A IVc.iv.11)

nṯk   G bite (In I.22)
N bite each other (B VI.vi.19)

nṯq   armour-bearer (B IV.vii.39)

s

sʾin   hem (B VI.ii.10)

sʾd   D sustain, regale (B I.i.3)

s³d see *s ͨd*

sb G 1. go round (B V. vi.3)

  2. turn into (B IV.vi. 34)

  N be turned into (B IV. vi.35)

sbb see *sb*

sgr G lock (K I.ii.43)

sgrt lockable room (B I.v. 12)

sd company (A IVb.i.4)

sdn Sidannu (PN, spirit) (R II.6)

shr D go round (A IVb.ii. 11)

sk vest (K III.ii.31)

sk lair (In III.4)

skn Gp be shaped (B IV.i. 42)

  S shape, construct (B IV.i.20)

skn stele (A I.i.26)

skn moment, right time (MR II.ii.52)

skt construction (B II.iii.8)

slm staircase (R III.21)

sm drug (A III.iv.61)

sm scarlet, purple (A IVc. iv.19)

smkt height (K III.i.35)

sml shape (A I.vi.11)

smm perfume (K III.iii.10)

snnt swallow (A I.ii.27)

ssw horse (K I.i.48)

ssn date-cluster (MR VI. 66)

s ͨd N be regaled (A IVb. i.2)

s ͨd see *s³d*

s ͨy G assault (K I.iii.7)

sp bowl (K I.iii.44)

sp³ G feed, serve food (A I.i.31)

  N be fed, eat (B V. i.5)

spd G beat the breast (K III.ii.27)

  S pound the breast (A III.iv.10)

spsg glaze (A I.vi.36)

spr G count (B VI.vi.37)

  N be counted (B IV. viii.8)

  D recite (MR I.57)

  S make count (A I.vi. 28)

spr scribe (B VI.vi.54)

spr 1. enumeration (K I.ii. 37)

  2. list (B II.ii.5)

  3. report (R II.1)

sr   D fly (K I.ii.17)

srn   ruler (A IVc.iv.18)

srr   see *sr*

str   G/D hide (B IV.vii.48)

ꜥ

ꜥ*bd*   G work, serve (B I.i.2)

ꜥ*bd*   slave (B III.i.36)

ꜥ*bṣ*   G make haste (B I. iii.18)

ꜥ*br*   G pass (B I.vi.4)

ꜥ*gl*   bull-calf (B I.iii.44)

ꜥ*glt*   heifer (B V.v.18)

ꜥ*gm*   angry cry (K I.i.27)

ꜥ*gml*   ꜥAgmalu (monster) (R I.9)

ꜥ*d*   to, until (B V.vi.4)

ꜥ*d*   G return (A III.iv.26) Lt recount (B IV.iii.11)

ꜥ*d*   again (B IV.iii.40)

ꜥ*d*   company (B VI.vi.48)

ꜥ*d*   time (MR II.ii.45)

ꜥ*d*   dais (K III.vi.22)

ꜥ*db*   G 1. put, place (B II.ii. 10)
    2. make, prepare (A I.v.16)
    3. handle, poise (B VI.i.51)

ꜥ*db*   see ꜥ*ḏb*

ꜥ*dbt*   furnishings (B IV.vi. 38)

ꜥ*dd*   courier (B IV.vii.46)

ꜥ*dd*   see ꜥ*d*

ꜥ*dy*   D remove (MR VI.66) S drive away (K III.v. 41)

ꜥ*dm*   G disappear (R II.17)

ꜥ*dm*   see ꜥ*d*

ꜥ*dn*   time (B IV.v.6)

ꜥ*dn*   D appoint the time (B IV.v.7)

ꜥ*dn*   host, army (K I.ii.32)

ꜥ*dn*   bottom of a bucket (K III.iii.14)

ꜥ*dt*   1. assembly (K III.v.5)
    2. confluence (MR VI.3)

ꜥ*dt*   1. time (MR I.67)
    2. menstruation (In I.1)

ꜥ*dt*   scab, lichen (MR VI. 66)

ꜥ*ḏb*   G put down (MR II.ii. 26)

ꜥ*ḏbt*   merchandise (B IV.v. 14)

ꜥ*ḏr*   G help (A II.i.14)

ꜥ*wd*   see ꜥ*d*

ꜥ*wp*   see ꜥ*p*

ꜥ*wr*   blind (A III.iv.5)

ꜥ*wr*   see ꜥ*r*

ˤz   G be strong (B III.iv.17)

ˤz   strong (B VI.vi.17)

ˤz   strength (In V.21)

ˤzz   see ˤz

ˤṭr   primrose (K III.v.44)

ˤṭrṭrt   fragrant herb (K III. iii.11)

ˤṭrt   crown (B III.iv.37)

ˤẓm   bone (A III.iii.5)

ˤẓm   force (B III.iv.5)

ˤẓm   strong, mighty (B I.i. 12)

ˤẓm   strongly, mightily (MR II.i.24)

ˤyn   see ˤn

ˤl   1. on, up, by, against (B Ia.7; I.i.21)
   2. because of (B VI.v.11)

ˤl   above (adv.) (A I.ii.9)

ˤl   N suck (L II.iii.25)

ˤl   child (B VI.iv.19)

ˤlg   D stammer (In III.11)

ˤly   G go up, ascend (B IV. i.23)
   D bring up (B V.iv.20)
   S 1. make rise (A III.ii. 39)
      2. make mount (B V. v.21)
   St push oneself up, arch up (acrobat?) (MR I.31)

ˤly   height (MR I.2)

ˤly   over (R I.37)

ˤly   most high (K III.iii.6)

ˤll   see ˤl

ˤllmy   usurper (A IVc.iii.12)

ˤllmn   usurper (B II.iv.5)

ˤlm   eternity (B I.v.31)

ˤlm   on the following day (R I.8)

ˤln   above (B I.iii.34)

ˤlṣ   jubilant cry (B III.i.12)

ˤm   with, to, as, like (B I.iii. 19; iv.37)

ˤm   clan (A I.i.27)

ˤm   D make dark (B IV.vii. 55)

ˤmd   G approach (In III.3)
   D place, position (B III.iii.12)

ˤmm   whole body (A III.i.9)

ˤmm   see ˤm

ˤmn   with, to, towards (B I. iii.25; V.v.20)

ˤms   G carry (B IV.v.11)
   D hoist, support (A I.i. 30)

ˤmq   plain, valley (B I.ii.6)

ˤmq   strong (A I.vi.45)

ˤmr   sheaf (B V.vi.14)

ˤmrpˀi   ˤAmmurapi (PN) (R II.31)

ˤmt   G roll up (K III.vi.8)

ᶜmṯtmr ᶜAmmithtamru (PN, spirit) (R II.11)

ᶜn 1. eye (B Ia.5)
    2. metaph. source (MR II.ii.59)
    3. metaph. bubble (B VI.iv.18)
    4. metaph. vulva (MR V.8)

ᶜn G see, eye (B I.i.15)
    Gt eye each other (B VI.vi.16)

ᶜn furrow (K III.iii.4)

ᶜny G answer, speak (B I.iv.5)

ᶜny G be humbled (K III.vi.58)

ᶜny wretched (K III.ii.30)

ᶜnn clouds (L II.ii.33)

ᶜnn attendant (B I.iv.32)

ᶜnq necklace (A IVc.iv.19)

ᶜnt now (A III.iii.48)

ᶜnt furrow (B VI.iv.1)

ᶜnt ᶜAnatu (goddess) (B I.ii.4)

ᶜsy G do (B IV.iv.34)

ᶜsy see also ᶜšy

ᶜp G fly (A III.iii.44)
    L charm (B IV.ii.10)

ᶜp flight (L II.ii.11)

ᶜp bird (A II.iv.42)

ᶜpᶜpm du. eyelashes (K I.iii.43)

ᶜpr dust, ground (B I.iv.9)

ᶜpr D throw up dust (MR II.i.24)

ᶜprt dust, ground (B I.iii.15)

ᶜpt coll. birds (A IVc.iv.11)

ᶜṣ tree, wood, shaft (B Ia.4)

ᶜṣ G press on (B I.iii.18)

ᶜṣp reaped corn (In IV.7)

ᶜṣṣ see ᶜṣ

ᶜṣr bird (B I.iv.1)

ᶜq eye-shadow (K I.iii.43)

ᶜq see ᶜqq

ᶜqb heel, hock (A I.vi.23)

ᶜqb D oppose (A II.i.19)

ᶜqltn coiling (B I.iii.41)

ᶜqq ripper (monster) (MR II.i.27)

ᶜqšr having sloughed its skin (snake) (MR VI.5)

ᶜr N be aroused, awake (B VI.vi.31; MR III.28)
    L arouse (B IV.iv.39)

ᶜr city (B IV.vii.7)

ᶜr he-ass (B IV.iv.4)

ᶜrb G 1. enter (B I.iii.9)
        2. set (sun) (R I.47)

S make enter (K I.iv. 41)

ʿrb Arab, bedouin-warrior (MR I.7)

ʿrgz jujube-tree (A IVb.i.8)

ʿrw see ʿry

ʿrẓ rich (B VI.i.54; MR II. ii.30)

ʿry Gp be denuded, wiped out (K I.i.7)

ʿrym nakedly (K III.ii.29)

ʿrk G lay out orderly (MR III.29)

ʿrm nakedness (In III.13)

ʿrs D celebrate a wedding (A II.iv.15)

ʿrs see also ʿrš (cf. the parallel ʿsy/ʿšy)

ʿrʿr tamarisk (MR VI.64)

ʿrp D break the neck (In II.4)

ʿrpt cloud (B I.ii.40)

ʿrš bed (K III.vi.36)

ʿrš see also ʿrs

ʿšy G do, make (A I.i.29)

ʿšy see also ʿsy

ʿšr G prepare a banquet (B I.i.9)
N be served a banquet (A I.vi.30)

ʿšr banquet (R III.2)

ʿšr ten (R I.22)

ʿšr tenth (A I.ii.45)

ʿšr D pay the tithe (R IV. 32)

ʿšrm twenty (R I.43)

ʿšrt banquet (K II.ii.8)

ʿšrt ten (R I.3)

ʿšrt tithe (R IV.32)

ʿšty one (R II.27)

ʿtd D prepare (B V.iii.5)

ʿtk D attach (B I.ii.11)
N attach oneself to (K II.v.24)

ʿtq G pass (B II.ii.12)

ʿtqb ash-tree (MR IV.14)

ʿṯtr ʿAthtaru (god) (B III. iii.12)

ʿṯtrt ʿAthtartu (goddess) (B III.i.8)

ġ

ġb branches (MR II.ii.39)

ġbt milk (B Ia.8)

ġd D shake (B I.ii.25)

ġd see also ġḏ

ġdd see ġd

ġḏ G shake (B IV.vii.41)

ġḏ see also ġd

ġḏḏ see ġḏ

ġwy D pervert (In I.42)

ġz G be munificent (K III. vi.30)

ġzz see *ġz*

ġzr youth, hero (B I.i.20)

ġzy G seek favour, bribe (B IV.ii.11)

ġyr low realm (B II.iii.21)

ġyr see *ġr*

ġl marsh (A I.vi.23)

ġl D make enter (B I.ii.13)

ġly G sink down, wilt (A III.iii.54)

D let sink, lower (B I.i.1)

ġll after-thirst (A IVc.iv.19)

ġll very thirsty (MR II.ii.34)

ġll see *ġl*

ġlm G darken (K III.i.50)

ġlm darkness (B III.iii.11)

ġlm lad (B I.ii.4)

ġlmt darkness (B IV.vii.54)

ġlmt lass (K I.iv.41)

ġlp 1. sheath (A III.i.19)

2. with *ym*: murex brandaris, purple snail (A III.iv.42)

ġlt slackness (K III.vi.32)

ġm° G be thirsty (B IV.iv.34)

ġm° see also *zm°*

ġnb grape (A III.i.42)

ġnṯ G suck out (?) (In V.11)

ġṣr border (B IV.viii.4)

ġr G sink, cower (B III. iv.6)

ġr negligence (In IV.1)

ġr skin (B V.vi.17)

ġr mountain (B Ia.1)

ġrm G pledge (In I.5)

ġrm usurer (K III.vi.31)

ġrmn plane-tree (B I.ii.11)

ġrt rock (B II.iii.9)

ġtr D ask (B IV.iv.33)

p

p and then, well (B I.i.2)

p 1. mouth (B Ia.8)

2. metaph. counsel, order (B IV.vii.20)

3. metaph. vulva (MR IV.32)

4. metaph. edge (of sword) (B III.iv.5)

p°alt cracked land (A III.ii.12)

p°amt time (MR I.20)

p°amt see also *pᶜmt*

p°at 1. brow (B III.iii.12)

2. edge of region (MR I.68)

p²at see also *p²it*

p²id heart (B II.iii.22)

p²it 1. brow (A I.ii.9)
2. edge of tools (B III. iv.5)

p²it see also *p²at* and *pht*

pbl Pubala (PN) (K I.iii.15)

pg legion (In I.26)

pgl foul meat (B IV.iii.15)

pd lock of hair (A III.ii.31)

pdr city (B IV.vii.8)

pdr Pidru (god) (?) (B I.i. 25)

pdry Pidrayu (goddess) (B I. i.23)

pd̲ gold (B III.i.19)

phy G see, regard (B I.i.14)

pht pl. of *p* mouth

pwq see *pq*

ph̲l he-ass (B IV.iv.5)

ph̲lt she-ass (MR VI.1)

ph̲m coal (B IV.ii.9)

ph̲d ram, coll.stock (A I.v. 17)

ph̲yr whole assembly (K I.i. 25)

ph̲r assembly (B III.i.24)

ph̲r potter (L I.7)

pz̲ġ G bruise (A III.iv.11)

pl G crack (B VI.iv.1)

plg ditch (In I.24)

plg D flow freely (MR VI. 69)

plṭ D deliver (A II.i.13)

ply D make feel marvellous, stroke (B Ia.5)

plk spindle (B IV.ii.3)

pll see *pl*

plṭṭ wallowing (B V.vi.15)

pn prohibitive particle (MR III.12)

pn face, surface (B I.iv. 37)

pnw face, front (B I.i.6)

pny G turn to (L I.6)

pnm inside (K III.vi.5)

pnm see *pn*

pnn face, front (B I.iv.40)

pnt (1. cornerstone)
2. metaph. joint, vertebra (B I.iii.34)

pslt flint (B V.vi.18)

p²l work (MR IV.21)

p²mt time (R III.26)

p²mt see also *p²amt*

p²n foot (B I.iii.9)

p²nm barefoot (R III.24)

p²r G 1. open wide the mouth (MR IV. 32)
2. proclaim, give a name (B II.iv.15)

N be proclaimed (B II.
iv.13)

pġt 1. girl (K II.iii.6)
2. Pughatu (PN) (A III.
i.27)

ppšr Papsharru (god) (In I.
36)

ppšrt Papsharratu (goddess)
(In I.36)

pq G get, receive (B IV.iii.
41)
Gt appropriate (B II.v.
13)
S supply (B IV.vi.47)

pqd G summon (K III.vi.
14)

pqq node of plant (MR III.
30)

pr N fly, flap the wings
(B III.i.12)

pr fruit (B V.ii.5)

pr G break a vow (K II.iii.
29)

prbḫt Perubakhthi (goddess)
(MR V.49)

prgl Pirigalu (PN, god)
(R I.50)

prṭl hellebore (In I.7)

prln majordomo (B VI.vi.
55)

prs parasu-measure (R I.
23)

prsḥ N collapse (B III.iv.22)

prst decision (A IVc.iii.15)

prᶜ 1. first (A I.v.37)
2. top (A IVc.iv.24)

prᶜ sovereignty (B V.v.3)

prᶜ Dt make excellent,
beautify oneself (MR
IV.19)

prᶜt princess (B IV.vii.56)

prṣ breach (MR I.70)

prq G dissolve (B IV.iv.28)

prq cella (B II.v.13)

prr see *pr*

prš⁾ G cover (B IV.i.35)

prt young cow (B V.v.18)

pšᶜ transgression (A I.vi.
43)

ptḥ G open (B IV.vii.19)
N be opened (B IV.vii.
17)

ptḥ door (In I.21)

pty D seduce (MR I.39)

ṣ

ṣ⁾at outcome, rise (B I.ii.8)

ṣ⁾in small stock, sheep
(B IV.vi.41)

ṣb⁾ G set (sun) (A III.iv.47)

ṣb⁾u soldier, army (B I.ii.
22)

ṣbrt host (B I.v.37)

ṣd G scour, hunt (B V.vi. 26)

ṣd hunt (noun) (A I.v.37)

ṣd game (A IVc.iv.11)

ṣd G provide food (In V.12)

ṣdyn Sidonian (K I.iv.36)

ṣdq righteousness (K I.i.12)

ṣdr mind (In I.25)

ṣhl G radiate (A I.ii.9)

ṣwd see *ṣd*

ṣwḥ see *ṣḥ*

ṣḥ G cry (B I.iii.36)

ṣḥq G laugh (B IV.iv.28)

ṣḥq laughter (B I.ii.25)

ṣḥq see also *ẓḥq*

ṣḥr L become brownish, brown (B I.v.17)

ṣly D adjure, pray (A III.i. 39)

ṣlm image (MR I.57)

ṣlt prayer (R IV.34)

ṣm G strike with a stick (A III.iii.46)

ṣmd G 1. bind (MR I.10) 2. harness (B IV. iv.5)

ṣmd double axe (B VI.v.3)

ṣmdm du. double axe (B III. iv.10)

ṣml G (1. be hard) 2. abstain from food (In III.7)

ṣml Samlu (name of bird) (A III.iii.29)

ṣmm see *ṣm*

ṣmt G/D silence (B I.ii.8)

ṣ^c bowl (B I.ii.32)

ṣ^cṣ^c agitation (In I.18)

ṣ^cq G cry (A IVc.iv.28)

ṣġd G stride forward (L II. iii.7)

ṣġr small (B VI.v.4)

ṣġrt infancy (L II.iii.26)

ṣp clarity (K I.iii.45)

ṣpn Sapanu (mountain) (B Ia.2)

ṣpr G keep watch (K I.iii. 19) D keep watch (MR I. 25)

ṣṣt salt-marsh (In II.11)

ṣq S restrain (B VI.ii.10)

ṣq narrow (In I.25)

ṣq crest (A IVc.iv.25)

ṣqrn inhabitant of the Third Heaven (R I.50)

ṣr G harass (K I.iii.29)

ṣr anguish (MR IV.5)

ṣr Tyrian (K I.iv.35)

ṣrḥ comet (MR IV.14)

ṣrk G fail (A III.i.43)

ṣrr see *ṣr*

ṣrr young ear of corn (A III. i.17)

ṣrry heights (K III.i.5)

ṣrrt highlands (B I.i.21)

ṣrt opposition, foe (B I.iii. 37)

ṣt sackcloth (A I.i.4)

q

qbʾ G summon (B VI.vi.39)

qblbl headrest (B IV.i.36)

qbʿt goblet (A III.iv.54)

qbṣ gathering (K II.iii.4)

qbr G bury (B VI.i.17)

qbr grave (K III.ii.25)

qbt wine-sink (B VI.iv.18)

qd G cower (A IVc.iii.14)

qdd see *qd*

qdm 1. East (B IV.vii.40)
       2. Qadmu (god) (MR II.i.8)

qdm before (B I.iv.41)

qdm G proceed (K II.iv.23)
       D bring, offer (R II. 30)

qdmy ancient (B IV.vii.34)

qdqd skull (B I.v.24)

qdš holy (B I.i.13)

qdš 1. sanctuary (MR I.3)
       2. Qudshu (name of goddess Athiratu) (B III.i.38)

qdš S consecrate (R IV.30)

qdš wʿamrr Qidshu-and-Amruru (god) (B I.vi.11)

qwl see *ql*

qwm see *qm*

qwr see *qr*

qṭr smoke (A I.i.27)

qẓ summer fruit (A IVb. I.5)

qẓ exchange-marriage (MR V.2)

qẓb Sting (demon) (B V.ii. 23)

qym see *qm*

ql G fall (B I.iii.10)
     S 1. fell, slay (B II.iv.30)
        2. allow to fall (K III. vi.32)
     St proceed (B I.ii.18)

ql stupor (In I.28)

ql D curse (A I.vi.52)

ql voice (B I.i.20)

qll see *ql*

qlṣ D scoff, revile (B IV.iii. 12)

qlṣ scorn (B I.v.28)

qlt filth, abomination (B IV.iii.15)

qm G rise, stand (B I.i.4)
     D make stand up (A IVc.iv.5)

qmḥ   flour (R I.23)

qmṣ   G curl up (K I.i.35)

qmṣ   multitude (B II.iv.32)

qmṣ   see also *qnṣ*

qn   1. reed (A I.vi.23)
2. pipe (B IV.viii.20)
3. arrow (A I.vi.9)

qny   G 1. create, beget (B I.
v.9)
2. acquire, possess
(A III.iv.58)

qnṣ   Gt crouch (MR I.51)

qnṣ   see also *qmṣ*

qᶜl   1. hall (A IVc.iv.16)
2. Qaᶜilu (city) (B I.
vi.8)

qṣ   G slice up (B I.i.8)

qṣ   edge (B VI.ii.11)

qṣm   piece of bark of the
plane tree (B I.ii.10)

qṣᶜt   arrow (A I.v.3)

qṣṣ   see *qṣ*

qṣr   short (K III.vi.34)

qṣt   end, fringe (B V.vi.4)

qr   G twist, curve (A I.vi.
14)

qr   sound (K I.iii.16)

qr   G sprinkle (B V.ii.22)

qr   fountain (MR II.ii.60)

qr mym   Qoru-Mayima
(city) (A III.iii.45)

qrʾ   G 1. call, invite (B IV.
vii.47)
2. invoke (gods, spir-
its) (MR I.1)

qrb   G come near (B IV.viii.
16)
Pāᶜil draw near (K II.
iii.5)
D bring near (A II.i.25)
S bring near, offer
(K III.i.44)

qrb   near (B II.iv.2)

qrb   1. middle (B I.v.6)
2. euphem. abdomen
(L III.1)

qrd   hero (B I.iii.14)

qry   G meet (B I.ii.4)
D 1. bring, offer (A III.
iv.22)
2. oppose (B I.iii.1)

qryt   city (B I.ii.7)

qrn   1. horn (B Ia.6)
2. ray, flash (B I.iv.27)
3. cusp (A III.iv.10)

qrᶜ   rod (MR III.8)

qrṣ   G pinch (MR II.i.11)
D pinch off (K III.v.
29)

qrr   see *qr*

qrš   camp, fenced territory
(B I.v.8)

qrt   city (B I.ii.20)

qš   present (B I.v.33)

qšb   G listen (B II.ii.13)

qšr   G overpower (In I.20)

qšt   bow (B I.ii.16)

qt̠   G drag out (B III.iv.28)
        R tear out (MR III.5)

qt̠t̠   see *qt̠*

r

rʾim   beloved (B I.iii.4)

rʾiš   1. head (B Ia.5)
         2. top (MR III.30)
         3. first (R I.1)

rʾišy   former (R IV.25)

rʾiš yn   month name (R I.1)

rʾit̠   Riʾthu (god ?) (R I.36)

rʾu   appearance (B I.i.12)

rʾum   wild ox (B IV.i.43)

rb   mist, drizzle (B I.i.25)

rb   large, great, many (B I.i. 12)

rbb   drizzle (B I.ii.39)

rbbt   ten thousand (B IV.i. 28)

rbᶜ   fourth (B IV.vi.26)

rbᶜ   D do something for the fourth time (K III.v.16)
        S make four (A I.v.3)

rbᶜt   quarter (A III.ii.34)

rbṣ   G rest (B Ia.1)

rbt   lady (B I.iv.49)

rbt   ten thousand (B I.i.17)

rgm   G say, speak (B I.iii. 11)

rgm   word (B I.iii.20)

rdy   G harass (B II.ii.4)

rdmn   Radmanu (god ?) (B I.i.2)

rdn   Radanu (PN, spirit) (R II.6)

rwẓ   see *rẓ*

rwy   G refresh (K III.ii.12)

rwm   see *rm*

rḥ   1. wind (B II.ii.9)
        2. spirit (B IV.iii.8; B V. iv.3)

rḥ   scent (B I.ii.2)

rḥb   G be wide (B V.iii.2)

rḥb   wide (K III.i.9)

rḥbt   vase, basin (B IV.vi. 53)

rḥl   Gt ride (In I.35)

rḥm   1. womb (L II.iii.1)
         2. damsel (B VI.ii.5)

rḥm   D be compassionate (K III.i.33)

rḥm   du. mill (B VI.ii.34)

rḥmy   Rihmayu (epithet of ᶜAnatu) (K II.ii.6)

rḥṣ G wash (B I.ii.32)

Gt wash oneself (K I. ii.9)

rḥq G 1. be far away (K I. iii.28)

2. remove oneself (B IV.vii.5)

S remove (B I.iv.40)

rḥq remote, far (B I.iv.34)

rḥt palm of the hand (B IV. viii.6)

rḥm carrion vulture (In I. 37)

rḥnt compassion (B IV.v.5)

rḥp D hover (A II.iv.20)

rẓ G run (B VI.i.50)

rk G be soft, relent (B VI. v.9)

rkb G 1. ride (B I.ii.40)

2. straddle (K I.ii.21)

rky G bind (In I.10)

rkk see *rk*

rks G bind (In II.9)

rks girdle (B V.i.4)

rm G 1. be high (K II.iii. 13)

2. raise (K III.ii.26)

L set up (B II.iii.27)

rm high, loud (K III.ii.25)

rm exalted (B IV.vii.55)

rm Gt crawl, swarm (B III. iv.3)

rmm see *rm*

rmṣt roasted portion (R I. 18)

rn D rejoice (In I.6)

rnn see *rn*

rᶜ friend (A IVc.iv.27)

rᶜy shepherd (A IVa.ii.6)

rᶜkt biscuit (?) (R IV.2)

rᶜt wickedness (In III.20)

rᶜt thunder (B Ia.4)

rġb G be hungry (B IV.iv. 33)

D be very hungry (K II. i.1)

rġn G turn green (MR VI. 61)

rġt D suck (B IV.iii.41)

rpʾ G heal (A IVa.ii.5)

rpʾu healer, saviour, spirit (B VI.vi.46)

rpy Gt be loosened (B V. i.4)

rq sheet (B IV.vi.34)

rqd D dance (In V.5)

rqḥ perfume (R I.21)

rqṣ Gt leap off (B III.iv.13)

rqt temple (A III.ii.38)

rš G crush, destroy (K I.i. 10)

ršᶜ G transgress (In III.6)

ršp Rashpu (god) (K I.i.19)

ršš see *rš*

rtq   G be inaccessable (MR IV.24)

rtq   inaccessable (B IV.vii.33)

rṯ   silt, mud (K III.v.29)

rṯn   silt (B II.iv.9)

rṯt   net (B IV.ii.32)

š

š   ram (R I.5)

š'ir   flesh (B VI.ii.35)

š'b   G draw water (B VI.i.6; K I.iii.9)

š'y   G murder (A II.iv.23)

š'l   G ask (B II.v.12)
   N be asked (B Ia.8)

š'r   Gt stay behind (A II.iv.15)

šb   old man (B I.ii.16)

šbḥ   see *sph*

šby   captive (B III.iv.30)

šblt   ear of grain (A III.i.18)

šbm   Gt muzzle (B I.iii.40)

šbm   muzzle (In II.8)

šbny   Shubanite (gent.) (B VI.vi.54)

šbˁ   G be sated (B I.ii.19)

šbˁ   satiety (MR III.3)

šbˁ   seven (B Ia.3)

šbˁ   seventh (B IV.vi.32)

šbˁ   D do for the seventh time (K III.v.20)

šbˁd   seven times (MR I.12)

šbˁm   seventy (B IV.vi.46)

šbš   G covet (B III.iii.11)
   (D attract)

šbt   D make stop (In I.3)

šbt   grey hair (B I.v.25)

šgr   offspring, young of cattle (B V.iii.16)

šd   field (B I.iii.17)

šd   acre, surface measure (B I.iii.1)

šd   Shedu (spirit) (In V.12)

šdy   G pour (B VI.iv.18)
   Gt be poured (B VI.iv.25)

šdmt   terrace (B III.i.43)

šzr   rope (In I.11)

šḥ   G study (MR II.ii.12)

šḥy   Lt prostrate oneself (B I.iii.10)
   St be made bow down (In I.11)

šḥl   stream (B V.v.19)

šḥl   see also *šlḥ*

šḥr   (1. dawn)
   2. Shaharu (god) (MR II.i.7)

šḥt   shrub (MR VI.65)

šḫṭ   G slaughter (A II.iv.24)

šḫn N be hot (R II.18)
    D make feverish (MR II.ii.38)

šḫp beestings (L II.iii.25)

šyḫ see *šḫ*

šyr see *šr*

šyt see *št*

šk Gt harrow (B VI.iv.2)

škb G 1. lie down (A I.i.4)
    2. copulate (B V.v. 19)

škk see *šk*

škllt woman about to deliver (K III.ii.28)

škn G settle (K I.ii.51)
    Gt establish (B IV.vii. 44)

šknt neighbour (K III.ii.53)

škr G be generous (K I.ii.44)

škr drunkenness (MR III.4)

škrn drunkenness (A I.i.30)

šlḥ G send (B III.iii.24)
    D smelt (B IV.i.25)

šlḥ (1. stream)
    2. Shalhu (river of death) (K I.i.19)

šlyṭ tyrant (B I.iii.42)

šlm peace (R II.31)

šlm 1. pacification (B I.ii. 32)
    2. peace-gift (K I.iii. 26)
    3. peace-offering (R I.2)

šlm whole, in peace (B VI. iv.24)

šlm Shalimu (god) (MR I. 52)

šm 1. name (B II.iv.14)
    2. consort (K III.vi.56)

šmʾal left, left hand (B III.i. 40)

šmḫ G rejoice (B I.v.20)

šmḫt joy (B I.ii.26)

šmy celestial being (A III. i.2)

šmk Shamku (region) (L II. ii.13)

šmm heaven (B Ia.7)

šmn oil (B I.ii.31)

šmn oily, fat (K II.iv.4)

šmᶜ G 1. hear (B I.v.10)
    2. obey (A I.v.21)
    Gt listen (K III.vi.29)

šmrr poisonous (MR VI.4)

šmt fat (A III.iii.4)

šmt gold-colour (MR I.21)

šn tooth (MR II.ii.41)

šn D gnash the teeth (K III. i.13)

šnʾ G hate (B IV.iii.17)

šnw/y G leave (B I.iv.33)

šnm Shanuma (god) (MR III.19)

šnm pl. of *šnt*

šns D tuck up (B I.ii.12)

šnpt wave-offering (?) (R IV.13)

šnt year (B VI.v.9) pl. *šnt* and *šnm* (B I.v.8)

šnt sleep (A III.iii.45)

šnt pl. of *šn*

šᶜr hair, wool (A III.ii.2)

šᶜr barley (A III.i.29)

šᶜtqt Shaᶜtiqtu (healing spirit) (K III.v.41)

šp summit, bare hill (MR I. 2; L II.iii.12)

šph clan (B VI.i.30)

šph offspring (K I.iii.48)

špk G pour out (A I.vi.15)

špk effusion (B I.iii.3a)

špl G be low, lower oneself (MR I.32) D throw down (MR IV.4)

špl deep (B III.iii.9)

špr horn (In V.10)

špš 1. sun (B I.ii.8) 2. Shapshu (goddess) (B VI.i.11)

špšm at sunset (K I.iii.3)

špt lip (B Ia.9)

šqd G heed (In IV.4)

šqy G give to drink (B I.i.9) S give to drink (A I.ii. 33)

šqy cup-bearer (B V.iv.19)

šql see *ql*

šr G sing (B I.i.18)

šr singer (A III.i.7)

šr stalk (MR III.30)

šr navel-string (L II.iii.25)

šr Sharru (god, = Motu) (MR I.8)

šr leader (MR II.ii.50)

šrg fabrication (A I.vi.35)

šrg D fabricate lies (A I.vi. 34)

šry G 1. let loose (B IV.v.9) 2. advance against (K I.iii.6)

šryn Shiryon (mountain) (B IV.vi.21)

šrk G join as partner (K II.v.17)

šrᶜ upsurge (A III.i.45)

šrp G burn (B VI.ii.33)

šrp burnt-offering (R I.13)

šrr hard, arduous (A III.ii. 36)

šrr stalk (K III.v.48)

šrš root (A I.i.19)

ššrt   chain (B V.v.3)

št   G put, place (B I.ii.1)
   Gp be placed (B IV.iii. 14)

št   base (B I.ii.5)

št   lady (A II.iv.6)

šty   G drink (B IV.iii.16)

štm   G stop the mouth (B I. iii.40)

t

tʾant   groaning (B I.iii.24)

tʾinṭṭ   womenfolk (A I.vi. 40)

tʾunt   see *tʾant*

tbʾut   yield (K II.v.11)

tbꜥ   G 1. rise, depart (B III. iii.7)
   2. rebel (K I.i.14)

tbtḫ   resting-place (B IV.i. 29)

tgh   turning away, setting (sun) (K III.i.37)

tdmm   lewdness (B IV.iii.20)

tdrq   see *drq*

tḏmr   Tadmaru (?) (city) (MR I.4)

thm   flood (MR VI.1)

thmt   flood (B I.iii.25)

thm   message, decree (B I. iii.13)

tḥt   under, below, at the feet of (B I.ii.9)

tk   1. middle (B Ia.2)
   2. in the middle, right before (B I.iv.41)

tk   demon (MR II.i.20)

tkn   Dt be steadied (MR II. ii.57)

tl   mound (B IV.viii.4)

tlʾiyt   victory (B Ia.3)

tlm   furrow, ridge (K III.iii. 11)

tlꜥ   worm (B III.iv.4)

tlš   Tulishu (goddess) (MR II.i.14)

tm   totality (K I.i.24)

tm   complete, perfect (MR I.67)

tmn   (1. foundation-stone)
   2. pelvis (B III.iv.18)

tmnt   pelvis (In III.6)

tnmy   overflow (B II.iv.9)

tnn   Tunnanu (marine monster) (B I.iii.40)

tnqt   cry (K III.ii.26)

tnqt   nursing (MR IV.32)

tnr   L roast in the oven (R IV.9)

tsm loveliness (K I.iii.42)

t⁽ᶜ⁾dt envoy (B III.i.11)

t⁽ᶜ⁾lgt stammering (In IV.2)

t⁽ᶜ⁾rt pouch (A II.iv.18)

tġzyt presentation (B VI.vi. 45)

tp beauty (L I.2)

tp tambourine (In V.4)

tpḫ apple (A IVb.ii.11)

tq⁽ᶜ⁾t Taqi⁽ᶜ⁾atu (goddess) (MR V.49)

tr D make quake, make tremble (B IV.vii.31)

tr see *ntr*

trbṣ corral (K I.i.49)

trḫ D marry (K I.i.14)
Dp be married (K I.i. 13)

trḫ groom (K I.ii.47)

trẓẓ pool (K III.i.49)

trmmt cultic contribution (B VI.vi.44)

trmn Tarmennu (PN, spirit) (R II.5)

tr⁽ᶜ⁾ G pervade (MR II.ii.42)

trġzz Targhuzaz (mountain) (B IV.viii.2)

trr see *tr*

trṯ must (MR III.4)

tšyt triumph (B I.ii.27)

tš⁽ᶜ⁾m ninety (B IV.vii.12)

ttl Tuttul (city) (MR VI. 15)

ṯ

ṯ'at ewe (In IV.8)

ṯ'igt roaring (K I.iii.16)

ṯ'iṭ loam (B II.iv.8)

ṯ'iqt see *ṯ'igt*

ṯ'ir groomsman (A II.i.25)

ṯ'r G 1. arrange (B I.ii.37)
   2. make arrangements (B III.iii.16; see *ṯ'ir*)
   3. procure (K I.i.15)

ṯ'r see also *ṯ'r*

ṯb G 1. return (B I.iv.54)
   2. do again (B I.iv. 21)
   3. reply (B III.i.6)
D restore (In IV.3)
L turn repeatedly (In III.19)
S 1. send back (MR III. 27)
   2. reply (B III.iii.23)

ṯbr G 1. break (K III.i.54)
   2. come loose (B I. iii.33)
N be broken (A III.i.4)
D crush (B III.i.7)

_t_br molar, jaw, bill (B III.i. 13)

_t_brn molars, jaws (B IV. viii.19)

_t_bš D give substance (A IVc.iv.6)

_t_bt dwelling (B II.iii.9)

_t_bt see _y_tb

_t_d 1. teat, breast (MR IV. 19)
     2. udder (L II.iii.20)

_t_d suckling (B I.i.6)

_t_dt sixth (B IV.vi.29)

_t_dt D do for the sixth time (K III.v.19)

_t_wb see _t_b

_t_wy (G stay)
     D allow to stay (K III. vi.31)

_t_wr see _t_r

_t_kḫ G uncover, strip (MR V.4; L III.1)
     N be uncovered (B V. i.4)

_t_kl G remain childless (MR VI.61)

_t_kl bereavement (MR I.8)

_t_kl Thukala (city) (MR I. 74)

_t_km 1. shoulder (A IVc.iv. 5)

     2. metaph. parapet (K I.ii.22)

_t_km G carry on the shoulder (A III.ii.1)

_t_kmn Thakumanu (god) (MR III.18)

_t_kr S bring tribute (K II. i.3)

_t_kt barque (B IV.v.7)

_t_lb shawm (In V.4)

_t_lḫn table (B I.ii.21)

_t_lḫḫ Thillukhuha (goddess) (MR V.47)

_t_lt three (B I.iv.36)

_t_lt third (B IV.vi.26)

_t_lt D do for the third time (B V.vi.20)

_t_lt bronze (bolt) (MR VI. 71)

_t_ltʾid three times (A II. iv.23)

_t_ltm thirty (R I.19)

_t_ltt three times (K III.v.9)

_t_m G/D be horrified (B V. iii.13)

_t_m there (B III.iv.4)

_t_mk Thamuka (region) (A IVc.iv.17)

_t_mm see _t_m

_t_mn there (A III.i.5)

_t_mn eight (B Ia.4)

tmn   Dt do eight times (K II. ii.24)

tmnym   eighty (B IV.vii.11)

tmq   G rise up high (A IVc. iv.8)

_tn_   two (B I.iv.35)

_tn_   second (B IV.vi.24)

_tn_   scarlet (MR I.22)

tny   G repeat (B I.iii.12)
D do for the second time (K III.v.13)
Dt do again (B V.iv.19)

tnm   twice (A II.iv.22)

tnn   trooper, life-guard (K I. ii.38)

tnnt   twice (K III.v.8)

tnt   urine (MR III.21)

_tᶜ_   nobleman (K I.i.51)

_tᶜ_   oblation (R IV.11)

tᶜy   G offer (R II.27)

tᶜy   officiant (B VI.vi.57)

tᶜr   G arrange, stack (B I. i.4)

tġr   gate, door (B I.ii.3)

tġr   gate-keeper (MR III.11)

tpd   G position, place (B IV. iv.29)

tpṭ   G judge, rule (A I.v.8; B I.v.32)

tpṭ   lawsuit (A I.v.8)

tpṭ   judge, ruler, see _tpṭ_ G.

tpz   see _tpṭ_

tṣr   ambrosia (A IVb.ii.11)

tqb   ash-tree (A I.vi.20)

tql   G weigh (A III.ii.34)

tql   shekel (weight) (K I.i. 29)

_tr_   bull (B I.iv.54)

_tr_   Tharru (PN, spirit) (R II.7)

_tr_   G espy, watch (B I.v. 13)

tryl   Tharyelli (PN) (R II.7)

trm   G 1. cut up meat (In I.8)
2. dine (K III.vi.18)

trm   banquet (B Ia.8)

trmg   Tharrumag (mountain) (B IV.viii.3)

trml   frothing milk (K I.iii. 44)

trmn   Tharrumannu (god) (K II.ii.4; B VI.vi.59)

trr   small (K I.iii.5)

trry   fem. of _trr_

_tš_   robber (K III.vi.48)

ttmnt   Thatmanatu (PN) (K II.iii.12)

ttᶜ   G dread, fear (B I.v.16; V.ii.7)

ttqt   Thatiqatu (goddess) (MR V.48)

_tt_   six (B IV.vii.9)

ttm   sixty (B IV.vii.9)

SEMANTIC GLOSSARY

Preliminary remarks:
1. The arbitrary nature of any division into semantic categories should be taken into account when using this glossary.
2. It should be realized that only the texts selected for CARTU are covered.

Overview of semantic spheres:

1. Existence – identity
2. Quantity – number
3. Quality
4. Relation – change – causation
5. Motion
6. Non-motion – rest
7. Time
8. Space
9. Unity – joining – binding – closing
10. Division – cutting – piercing – opening
11. Creation
12. Cosmology – astronomy
13. Geology – geography
14. Meteorology
15. Hydrology
16. Fire – light – darkness – colour
17. Flora (see also 39)
18. Fauna (see also 40,41)
19. Man – male
20. Woman – female
21. Body
22. Life – spirit – soul – awareness
23. Volition – motivation
24. Intelligence – memory
25. Vision
26. Taste
27. Smell – fragrance
28. Sound
29. Communication – speech – naming – writing
30. Food (see also 39-41)
31. Drink (see also 39,40)
32. Clothing
33. Cosmetics – hygiene
34. Jewelry (see also 44)
35. Habitation
36. Furniture
37. Receptacles – vessels
38. Work (general)
39. Agriculture
40. Cattle-breeding – domestic animals
41. Fishing – hunting
42. Trade – transportation
43. Technology – tools

44. Materials – minerals
45. Measuring
46. Art – music
47. Army – warriors
48. Weapons
49. Safety – protection
50. Happiness
51. Love – marriage – childbirth
52. Social relations – family
53. Law – ethics – sin – pity
54. Authority – power
55. Possession – wealth
56. Subjection – obedience
57. Courtesy – honouring – greeting
58. Gifts – tribute – taxes
59. Poverty – need
60. Animosity – danger – war (see also 46, 48)
61. Fear
62. Suffering – lament
63. Disease – medicine
64. Death – burial – mourning
65. Gods
66. Goddesses
67. Divine epithets
68. Minor deities – demons – monsters – spirits
69. Holy places
70. Cultic functionaries
71. Revelation
72. Cult – ritual
73. Sacrifice – offering
74. Vows
75. Magic
76. Prayer
77. Blessing – cursing

1. Existence – identity

ʾadm – ʾay – ʾal – ʾan – ʾank – ʾat – ʾatm – ʾin – ʾiṯ – ʾbd – ʾmr – ʾnš – bddy – bl – blt – hw – hwt – hy – hyt – hlk – hm – hmt – hndt – hpk – zr – ḥwy – ḥy – ḥym – ḫlq – ypʿ – kly – kn – l – lbd – m – mh – my – mn – mndʿ – mnm – mt – nbṭ – nḥn – npš – sml – ʿdm – pn – ṣrk – rʾu – škn – ṯbš

2. Quantity – number (see also 45)

ʾaḥd – ʾaḥdh – ʾalp – ʾarbʿ – ʾirby – ʾrk – bddy – gdl – gdlt – gmḏ – dq – dqt – ḏd – hg – hmlt – ḥbl – ḥyl – ḫl – ḥsn – ḥṣ – ḥmš – ḥmšt – ydt – kbd – kl – klʾat – kly – klt – kmm – lbd – mʾad – mʾat – mʾid – mʾit – mʾud – mʾd – md – mlʾ – mlʾu – mll – mn – mnt – mʿk – mṯn – nb – spr – ʿdn – ʿdt – ʿšr – ʿšrt – ʿšty – pʾamt – pg – pḫyr – pḫr – pʿmt – prʿ – ṣbʾu – ṣbrt – ṣġr – ṣq – qbṣ – qmṣ – qṣr – rʾiš – rb – rbbt – rbʿ – rbʿt – rbt – rḥb – rm – šbʿ – šbʿd – šbʿm – tm – tnmy – tšʿm – ṯb – ṯdṯ

– *ṯlṯ* – *ṯlṯ'id* – *ṯlṯm* – *ṯlṯt* – *ṯmn* – *ṯmnym* – *ṯn* – *ṯny* – *ṯnm* – *ṯnnt* – *ṯql* – *ṯrr* – *ṯt* – *ṯtm*

3. Quality

'abyn – *'adr* – *'ay* – *'al'iyn* – *'ib* – *brr* – *dk* – *dl* – *dn* – *dq* – *hyn* – *ḥdṯ* – *ḥzt* – *ḥpn* – *ḥbl* – *ḥḥ* – *ḥr* – *ṭb* – *ṭhr* – *ṭry* – *ẓhr* – *ysm* – *ysmsmt* – *ysmt* – *yp* – *ypy* – *yqr* – *kbd* – *kn* – *kṯr* – *l'y* – *mgṯ* – *mḥmd* – *mḫ* – *ngṯ* – *nsy* – *n'm* – *n'mn* – *'z* – *'zm* – *'ly* – *'mq* – *'ny* – *ġr* – *pgl* – *ply* – *pr'* – *ṣp* – *qdš* – *rk* – *rm* – *šmn* – *špl* – *šrr* – *tm* – *tsm* – *tp*

4. Relation – change – causation

'aḥdh – *'aḫr* – *'ap* – *'apn* – *'apnk* – *'aṯr* – *'ik* – *'im* – *'u* – *b* – *bl* – *bn* – *b'd* – *gm* – *d* – *dm* – *dt* – *hm* – *hpk* – *w* – *wn* – *ḫdṯ* – *yd* – *k* – *kd* – *km* – *kmm* – *kn* – *l* – *lm* – *m* – *mh* – *my* – *mn* – *mnt* – *'d* – *'l* – *'ly* – *'ln* – *'m* – *'mn* – *ġwy* – *p* – *šrk* – *tḥt*

5. Motion (see also more specific rubrics)

'ḥd – *'ḫr* – *'pq* – *'rḥ* – *'ty* – *'ṯr* – *b'* – *bhṯ* – *b'r* – *bqṯ* – *brḥ* – *brk* – *bš* – *ġhṯ* – *gl* – *gly* – *gmḏ* – *gr* – *gry* – *grš* – *d'y* – *dbr* – *dd* – *dlp* – *d'ṣ* – *dry* – *drk* – *drq* – *hbr* – *hlk* – *hlm* – *hpk* – *ḥbṯ* – *ḥbq* – *ḥsp* – *ḥr* – *ḥš* – *ḥt* – *ḥl* – *ḥš* – *ḥt'* – *ṭbḥ* – *ṭbq* – *ṭhn* – *ṭḫ* – *ṭlb* – *ṭ'n* – *ṯrd* – *zš* – *ybl* – *ydy* – *ydn* – *yḥy* – *yz'* – *ymn* – *ysd* – *yp'* – *yṣ'* – *yṣb* – *yṣq* – *yṣr* – *yrd* – *yry* – *ytn* – *yṯb* – *yṯq* – *kl'* – *kms* – *ksy* – *kry* – *l* – *l'k* – *lbn* – *lbš* – *lwy* – *lsm* – *lsmt* – *lqḥ* – *lṯ* – *md* – *mdl* – *mḥy* – *mḫy* – *mḥṣ* – *mḥš* – *mk* – *ml* – *ml'* – *msk* – *mġy* – *msḫ* – *mr* – *mrg* – *mšḫ* – *mšr* – *mt'* – *mtr* – *mṯk* – *nb* – *ngh* – *ngy* – *ngš* – *ngṯ* – *nd* – *ndp* – *nḥy* – *nḥt* – *nṭ* – *mṭm* – *nzp* – *nky* – *nkr* – *ns* – *nsy* – *nsk* – *ns'* – *n'r* – *ngš* – *npl* – *nṣ* – *nṣb* – *nqp* – *nš'* – *nšq* – *ntk* – *ntr* – *nṯk* – *sb* – *sgr* – *shr* – *skn* – *s'y* – *spd* – *'bṣ* – *'br* – *'d* – *'db* – *'dd* – *'dy* – *'dm* – *'ḏb* – *'l* – *'ly* – *'m* – *'md* – *'mn* – *'ms* – *'mt* – *'p* – *'pr* – *'ṣ* – *'r* – *'rb* – *'rp* – *'šy* – *'šr* – *'td* – *'tk* – *'tq* – *ġd* – *ġḏ* – *ġl* – *ġly* – *ġr* – *pzġ* – *pl* – *plg* – *ply* – *plṯṯ* – *pny* – *p'r* – *pr* – *prsḥ* – *pršʾ* – *ptḥ* – *ṣd* – *ṣmd* – *ṣġd* – *qbr* – *qd* – *qdm* – *ql* – *qm* – *qmṣ* – *qnṣ* – *qṣ* – *qr* – *qrb* – *qry* – *qrṣ* – *qšr* – *qṯ* – *rhl* – *rḥṣ* – *rḥq* – *rḥp* – *rz* – *rkb* – *rky* – *rks* – *rm* – *rpy* – *rqd* – *rqṣ* – *rš* – *šʾb* – *šbm* – *šdy* – *šhy* – *šhṯ* – *škb* – *škn* – *šlḥ* – *šnw/y* – *šns* – *šnpt* – *špk* – *špl* – *šry* – *šr'* – *št* – *štm* – *tb'* –

tgh – *tr* – *trᶜ* – *t̠ʾr* – *t̠b* – *t̠br* – *t̠kḫ* – *t̠km* – *t̠kr* – *t̠mq* – *t̠ᶜy* – *t̠ᶜr* – *t̠pd* – *t̠ql* – *t̠rm*

6. Non-motion – rest

ʾit̠ – *dmy* – *yšn* – *ytb* – *kḫt̠* – *ksʾu* – *kn* – *mt̠t* – *mnḫ* – *mškb* – *mtn* – *ln* – *nhmmt* – *nḫ* – *nḫt* – *nᶜl* – *ᶜmd* – *ᶜrš* – *qblbl* – *qmṣ* – *rbṣ* – *tbt̠ḫ* – *t̠bt* – *t̠wy*

7. Time

ʾaḫr – *ʾamd* – *ʾap* – *ʾaphn* – *ʾapn* – *ʾapnk* – *ʾat̠ryt* – *ʾibᶜlt* – *ʾid* – *ʾidk* – *ʾitml* – *ʾuḫryt* – *bḫt̠* – *bkm* – *dqn* – *drdr* – *hm* – *ht* – *ḥdt̠* – *ḥš* – *yḥy* – *ym* – *yṣʾ* – *yrḫ* – *k* – *kd* – *kly* – *km* – *l* – *llt* – *ln* – *lsm* – *lsmt* – *md* – *mk* – *mtn* – *nᶜr* – *nqpnt* – *nqpt* – *skn* – *ᶜbṣ* – *ᶜd* – *ᶜdn* – *ᶜdt* – *ᶜlm* – *ᶜnt* – *ᶜṣ* – *p* – *pʾamt* – *pᶜmt* – *qdm* – *qdmy* – *rʾišy* – *šb* – *šnm* – *šnt* – *špšm* – *t̠b* – *t̠ny*

8. Space (see also 12, 13)

ʾaḫr – *ʾap* – *ʾi* – *ʾiy* – *ʾuḫry* – *ʾḫd* – *bdq* – *bn* – *bᶜd* – *bᶜdn* – *d̠rᶜ* – *ḥwt* – *ẓr* – *ymn* – *ytn* – *kbd* – *mk* – *mnḫ* – *mqm* – *ᶜl* – *ᶜln* – *ᶜmd* – *pʾat* – *pʾit* – *pn* – *pnm* – *pnn* – *ṣq* – *qdm* – *qṣ* – *qrb* – *rḥq* – *rm* – *šd* – *šmʾal* – *špl* – *št*

9. Unity – joining – binding – closing

ʾahd – *ʾahdh* – *ʾiṣr* – *ʾzr* – *ʾḫd* – *ʾsp* – *ʾsr* – *bddy* – *gpn* – *ḥbl* – *ḥbq* – *ḥbš* – *ḥgr* – *ṭbq* – *ydt* – *ytq* – *kl* – *klʾat* – *klʾ* – *kly* – *klt* – *lbd* – *nqbn* – *sgr* – *sd* – *str* – *ᶜd* – *ᶜdt* – *ᶜtk* – *pḫyr* – *pḫr* – *ṣmd* – *qmṣ* – *qrṣ* – *rks* – *rtq* – *šbm* – *šzr* – *štm* – *tm*

10. Division – cutting – piercing – opening

bdq – *bdqt* – *bn* – *bqᶜ* – *brd* – *btl* – *glḥ* – *hdy* – *ḥz* – *ḥrb* – *ḥrt̠* – *ḫlpn* – *ṭᶜn* – *ydy* – *yᶜr* – *ktp* – *mšr* – *mtr* – *nqb* – *nt̠k* – *p* – *pʾalt* – *pl* – *pslt* – *prṣ* – *prq* – *ptḥ* – *ṣmd* – *ṣmdm* – *qṣ* – *qṣᶜt* – *qt̠* – *rḥq* – *šn* – *t̠br* – *t̠brn* – *t̠rm*

11. Creation

bny – *bnt* – *ḥmr* – *yṣr* – *kn* – *lt̠* – *qny* – *qrṣ* – *t̠bš*

12. Cosmology – astronomy

ʾarṣ – gml – dmrn – hlk – ḥdt̠ – hmry – yrḫ – kbkb – kbkbt – kkb – mk – msdt – mʿrb – ġṣr – ṣʾat – ṣbʾ – ṣqrn – ṣrḫ – qṣt – šmm – špš – tgh – thm – thmt

13. Geology – geography (see also 15, 44)

ʾablm – ʾabn – ʾaḫ – ʾaklt – ʾaln – ʾamr – ʾap – ʾapq – ʾarṣ – ʾarr – ʾaršḫ – ʾi – ʾinbb – ʾiqnʾu – ʾirt – ʾišd – ʾugrt – ʾudm – ʾudr – ʾuġr – ʾupqt – bʾir – bbt – bdqt – bmt – gb – gbl – gbʿ – gp – gpt – dbr – drk – drkt – hdrʿy – hmry – hrnmy – ḥkpt – ḥmr – ḥṣ – ḥryt – ḫbl – ḫbr – ḫḫ – ḫlb – ḫp – ḫr – ḫry – ḫršn – t̠t – z̠z̠ – z̠r – ym – ymʾan – ysmt – yrk – yrt – kdrt – knrt – kptr – lbnn – ll – lrgt – mʾiyt – mdb – mdbr – mdrʿ – mhyt – mḫrt̠t – mḫnm – mknpt – mslmt – mr – mrym – mrmt – mrrt – mšmš – mt̠ḫ – mt̠pd – nhr – nḫl – np – npk – ntbt – smkt – ʿly – ʿmq – ʿn – ʿpr – ʿprt – ʿr – ʿt̠trt – ġyr – ġl – ġṣr – ġr – ġrt – pʾalt – pʾat – pʾit – pdr – prʿ – ṣpn – ṣṣt – ṣq – ṣrry – ṣrrt – qdm – qʿl – qṣt – qr – qryt – qrn – qrt – rʾiš – rwy – rt̠ – rt̠n – šbny – šd – šdmt – šmk – šp – šryn – št – t̠dmr – tl – tr – trġzz – ttl – t̠kl – t̠mk – t̠rmg

14. Meteorology

ʾar – ʾipʾu – ʾiṣr – brq – glt̠ – gšm – ḥm – ḫd – ḫdd – t̠l – yr – lʾ – lḫ – mdl – mt̠r – nb – nskt – ʿnn – ʿrpt – s̠hr – rb – rbb – rwy – rḫ – rʿt – šrʿ – thm – thmt – t̠kt

15. Hydrology

ʾaḫ – ʾapq – ʾar – ʾaršḫ – ʾipʾu – ʾupqt – ʾpq – bʾir – bqr – br – brky – gb – gp – gšm – hlk – ḥsp – ḫp – t̠l – ym – yʿbdr – yṣq – kknt – lḫ – mʾiyt – mbk – mdb – mh – mhyt – mt̠r – my – mk – mm – mqr – mšmš – nb – nbk – nbʿ – nhr – nḫl – nzp – nsk – nskt – npk – ntk – ʿd – ʿdt – ʿn – ġl – plg – qr – rḥbt – šʾb – šdy – šḥl – šlḫ – špk – špl – šrʿ – thm – thmt – tnmy – trz̠z̠

16. Fire – light – darkness – colour

ʾagn – ʾargmn – ʾidm – ʾiqnʾu – ʾiš – ʾišt – ʾidm – ʾdm – ʾkl – ʾr – bʿr

– brq – dġt – ḏrq – ḥm – ḫtb – ḥr – z̧l – z̧lm – z̧lmt – yrq – kpr – lbn –
mdl – mᶜrb – nblʾat – nyr – nr – nrt – sm – ᶜm – ᶜmm – ᶜq – ᶜrb – ġlm
– ġlmt – pḥm – ṣʾat – ṣbʾ – ṣhl – ṣḥr – ṣp – qṭr – qrn – rġn – šḥr – šḫn
– šmt – špš – špšm – šrp – tnr – ṯn – ṯpd – ṯrml

17. Flora (see also 39)

ʾazmr – ʾannḫ – ʾarz – ʾaškrr – ʾib – ʾiln – ʾuṯkl – ʾur – ʾml – bnt – gb
– gd – gpn – ddy – zᶜtr – zt – ztr – ḥrnq – yblt – yᶜr – yrkt – kpr – kpt
– kš – kṯ – lb – lyt – lrmn – lty – ᶜdt – ᶜṭr – ᶜṭrṭrt – ᶜṣ – ᶜrgz – ᶜrᶜr –
ᶜṯqb – ġb – ġlp – ġrmn – pqq – prṭl – ṣḥr – srr – qn – qṣm – šḥt – šr –
šrr – šrš – ṯqb

18. Fauna (see also 40, 41)

ʾayl – ʾaylt – ʾanhb – ʾanḫr – ʾapᶜ – ʾarḫ – ʾarḫt – ʾibr – ʾinr – ʾirby –
ʾudn – bnt – bṯn – bṯnt – gmr – dʾiy – dʾit – dʾu – dʾy – dbb – dg – dgt
– ḏbb – ḏd – ḥbl – ḥwt – ḥmk – ḥsn – ḫt – ḫnzr – z̧by – yḥmr – yḫr – ynt
– yᶜl – knp – lbʾu – mn – ngr – ngrt – nḥš – nn – npr – nṣ – nšr – sk –
snnt – sr – ᶜlṣ – ᶜp – ᶜpt – ᶜṣr – ᶜqltn – ᶜqšr – ġlp ym – pr – rʾum – rḥm
– rḫp – rm – rqṣ – tlᶜ

19. Man – male (see also 47)

ʾab – ʾadm – ʾanšt – ʾaqht – ʾatn – ʾiḫ – ʾilḫʾu – ʾilmlk – ʾnš – bḥr – bkr
– bn – bnt – dkr – dnʾil – hrnmy – ḫpt – ḫr – yḥd – yṣb – yrgb – ytm –
khn – krt – krtn – kšp – mlk – mt – mṯ – nᶜr – nqd – nqmd – nšm – ᶜbd
– ᶜmrpʾi – ᶜmṯtmr – ᶜnn – ġzr – ġlm – pbl – ṣdyn – ṣr – rdn – šb – šbny
– trmn – ṯᶜ – ṯᶜy – ṯr – ṯrmn

20. Woman – female

ʾadt – ʾaḫt – ʾalmnt – ʾaṯt – ʾum – bkyt – bᶜlt – bt – btlt – dnty – ḫry –
ybmt – ybnt – ytmt – klt – mlkt – mrġt – mṯt – nᶜmy – ġlmt – pġt – prᶜt
– rbt – rḥm – škllt – št – tᶜinṯt – ṯtmnt – ṯryl

21. Body

ʾamt – ʾan – ʾanpn – ʾanš – ʾap – ʾaplb – ʾarkt – ʾirt – ʾišd – ʾišqb – ʾiṯl

– ʾudmᶜ – ʾudn – ʾuzᶜrt – ʾuṣbᶜ – ʾuṣbᶜt – ʾušk – bʾir – bd – bdq – bṭn
– bmt – brk – brlt – bšr – gb – gbtt – ggn – ǵd – gngn – grgr – dʾiy – dm
– dmᶜt – dᶜ – dqn – ḏd – ḏnb – ḏrᶜ – zd – ḥlq – ḥpn – ḫmt – ḫrʾu – ḫrzᶜ
– ṭmt – ẓr – yd – ydᶜ – ymn – yrk – kbd – klyt – knp – ksl – kp – ktp –
lb – lḥ – lṣb – lšn – mhmrt – mḫ – mḫlpt – mmᶜ – mnt – mpr – mrḥ –
mrrt – mtn – mtnm – nǵṣ – npš – nšb – ᶜdt – ᶜn – ᶜẓm – ᶜmm – ᶜn – ᶜpᶜpm
– ᶜqb – ᶜqšr – ᶜry – ᶜrym – ᶜrm – ᶜrp – ǵr – p – pʾat – pʾid – pʾit – pd
– pn – pnw – pnm – pnn – pnt – pᶜn – pᶜnm – qdqd – qn – qrb – qrn –
rʾiš – rḥm – rḫt – rqt – rtq – šʾir – šbt – šmʾal – šmn – šmt – šn – šᶜr
– špr – špt – šr – tmn – tmnt – ṯbr – ṯbrn – ṯd – ṯkm – ṯnt

22. Life – spirit – soul – awareness

ʾiṭ – ʾiṭl – blmt – brlt – ggn – ḥwy – ḥy – ḥym – ḥpn – ḫṭ – ysr – yqẓ –
kbd – lb – mpr – npš – nqh – ᶜr – rḥ

23. Volition – motivation

ʾagzr – ʾagzry – ʾal – ʾi – ʾhb – ʾrš – by – bǵy – bqṭ – gmr – hr – zd –
ḥmd – ḫṣ – ḫsr – ṭlb – ẓmʾ – ybl – ydn – ysr – ytn – k – kšd – l – mnt
– ᶜr – p – pn – prst – ql – rk – šbš – ṯb – ṯwy

24. Intelligence – memory

bkl – bn – dᶜt – hyn – hm – ḥkm – ḥkmt – ḫs – ydᶜ – ysr – yqǵ – lmd –
mlk – ngṯ – nšy – spr – ǵr – p – ṣdr – ṣq – ql – šḥ – šqd

25. Vision

ʾmr – bn – bṣr – bqṭ – gly – ḏhrt – ḏrt – hn – ḥdy – ḥlm – ṭlb – mẓʾ –
nbṭ – ngṯ – nǵr – ᶜn – ᶜr – phy – ṣd – rʾu – ṯr

26. Taste

brlt – ḥmṣ – ṭb – lḥk – mlḥ – mr – mtq – nbt – npš – ṣṣt

27. Smell – fragrance

ʾanpn – ʾap – ʾannḫ – gd – dǵt – dǵtt – zᶜtr – ztr – mr – mrḥ – nrd – smm
– ᶜtr – ᶜtrtrt – rḥ – rqḥ

28. Sound (see also 29, 46, 62, 64)

ʾg – ʾny – g – gl – gm – gᶜr – gᶜt – hm – zġy – zġt – ḥp – yb – kr – lḫš
– lḫšt – nhqt – nky – ᶜlṣ – ṣmt – ṣᶜq – qr – qšb – rm – rᶜt – šmᶜ – tʾant – ṯʾigt

29. Communication – speech – naming – writing

ʾamr – ʾap – ʾi – ʾimt – ʾu – ʾg – ʾmr – ʾrš – by – bġy – bšr – bšrt – g
– gl – gᶜr – dbr – ḥwt – hl – hlk – hlm – hln – ḫly – y – yb – yh – yqġ
– ytn – kny – l – lʾk – lḥ – lḫšt – lzt – lšn – mlʾak – mnt – mspr – mᶜ
– mšpy – nʾṣ – ngr – ngrt – nṣr – nqb – spr – ᶜgm – ᶜd – ᶜlg – ᶜny – ġtr
– p – pᶜr – pqd – sʾat – ṣḥ – qbʾ – ql – qlṣ – qrʾ – rgm – šʾl – šmᶜ – tḥm
– tnqt – tᶜdt – tᶜlgt – ṯb – ṯny

30. Food (see also 39, 40, 73)

ʾayl – ʾaylt – ʾakl – ʾišqb – ʾuṯkl – ʾkl – ʾpy – bly – blᶜ – brd – bšr – dbḥ
– znt – ḥtt – ḫt – ḥmʾat – ḥrṯ – ḥtʾ – ḫtr – ṯbḥ – ṯry – ṯt – ẓm – ydt –
yḥmr – kly – ksm – kš – ktp – kṯ – lḥm – mzn – mlḥ – mlḥmt – mll – mᶜk
– mġd – mṣd – mrʾ – mrʾu – mšt – nbt – ngb – npd – npš – nšb – nṯk –
sʾd – sᶜd – spʾ – ᶜdb – ᶜšr – ᶜšrt – pgl – pḥm – pq – pr – ṣd – šḥr – ṣml
– qmḥ – qṣ – qṯ – rmṣt – rᶜkt – rġb – šʾir – šbᶜ – šmn – šᶜr – tnr – tpḥ
– ṯʾiṭ – ṯṣr – ṯᶜr – ṯrm

31. Drink

ʾidm – dm – ḥlb – ḥsp – ḫlṣ – ḫmr – ṭb – ẓmʾ – yn – ynq – ks – krpn –
lḥ – mlʾ – mlʾu – msk – mṣ – mṣt – mrzḥ – mrzᶜ – mrṯ – mšt – nbt – nsk
– ntk – ᶜl – ᶜll – ġbt – ġll – ġmʾ – ġnṯ – qbᶜt – qbt – qlt – rwy – rġṯ –
rṯn – šʾb – šdy – šḫp – škr – škrn – špk – šqy – šty – tnqt – trṯ – ṯr

32. Clothing

ʾal – ʾall – ʾasr – ʾipd – ʾušpġt – ʾsr – bṣ – dbʾat – ḥbš – ḥgr – ḥtl – ksy
– kst – kpṯ – ktn – lbš – lpš – mʾizrtm – md – mdt – mks – npyn – npṣ
– npšn – nšg – sʾin – sk – ᶜr – ᶜrw – ᶜry – ᶜrym – ᶜrm – plk – ṣt – qṣ –
rks – šns – tᶜrt – ṯkḥ

33. Cosmetics – hygiene

ʾiqnʾu – ʾdm – brr – glḫ – dšn – hk – ḫbrṯ – ḫptr – yʿr – ypy – kpr – mḥy – ml – mr – mšḫ – nrd – smm – ʿq – prʿ – rḥṣ – rqḥ – šmn

34. Jewelry

ʾiqnʾu – ḫrṣ – yrq – ksp – ʿṯrt – ʿnq – ššrt

35. Habitation

ʾahl – ʾalt – ʾasm – ʾap – ʾarz – ʾiṣr – ʾugr – ʾudn – ʾulṯ – ʾurbt – bnwn – bny – br – bt – gb – gg – ggt – gdrt – grdš – dlt – ḏd – hkl – ḥdr – ḥzr – ḫl – ḫln – ḥmyt – ḥmt – ḫm – ḫmt – ḫšt – ṭḫ – ẓʾu – ydy – ysd – yṯb – kt – lbn – lbnt – mʾinš – mgdl – mẕll – mknt – mnḫ – msdt – mswn – msk – mslmt – mʿlt – mṣd – mṣr – mškn – mšknt – mṯb – mṯbt – nwt – sgr – sgrt – sk – skt – slm – ʿd – pnt – pʿl – prq – ptḥ – qʿl – qrš – rm – škn – tl – tmn – tmnt – ṯbt – ṯwy – ṯkm – ṯlṯ – ṯġr

36. Furniture

ʾaps – hdm – ḥdg – ḫym – ybl – yṯb – kḫṯ – kl – ksʾu – kt – mṭṭ – nḫt – nʿl – ʿd – ʿdbt – ʿrš – qblbl – rq – tbṯḥ – ṯʾr – ṯlḥn – ṯʿr

37. Receptacles – vessels

ʾagn – bk – ggn – gl – gngn – dd – dkrt – dn – ḥmt – ḫbrṯ – ḫptr – ṭbq – kd – kknt – kl – knkn – ks – kp – krpn – kṯ – mznm – mṭṭnt – mṣlt – mṣrp – mšg – sp – ʿdn – ġlp – ṣʿ – qbʿt – qbt – qn – rḥbt – špr – tʿrt – ṯpd

38. Work (general)

ʾamt – bny – bʿl – mʿll – skn – skt – ʿbd – ʿdb – ʿsy – ʿšy – pʿl

39. Agriculture

ʾazmr – ʾaklt – ʾasm – ʾib – ʾuṯkl – ʾml – ʾsp – bṣql – bqʿ – gdrt – gn – gpn – grn – dgn – dry – drk – drʿ – dṯ – zbr – zt – ḥṯṯ – ḥmdrt – ḥmṣ – ḥpš – ḥrb – ḥrṯ – ḥsp – ḫrb – ḫṯr – ṯḥn – ybl – yn – yġl – kbrt – ksm – kry – krm – kš – kṯ – lrmn – mʾiyt – mdrʿ – mhyt – mḥrṯṯ – mṭʿt – mn

– *mtr* – *nḥy* – *nsˁ* – *nˁr* – *nrt* – *sb* – *ˁmr* – *ˁn* – *ˁnt* – *ˁpr* – *ˁṣp* – *ġly* – *ġnb* – *pʾalt* – *pl* – *plg* – *pr* – *ṣmd* – *ṣmdm* – *ṣrr* – *qbt* – *qẓ* – *qmḥ* – *rwy* – *rḥm* – *šblt* – *šd* – *šdmt* – *šk* – *šˁr* – *šrp* – *tbʾut* – *tlm* – *tpḥ*

40. Cattle-breeding – domestic animals

ʾal – *ʾalp* – *ʾarḫ* – *ʾarḫt* – *ʾatnt* – *ʾibr* – *ʾil* – *ʾimr* – *ʾinr* – *ʾiṯm* – *bhm* – *bkr* – *gbṯt* – *gdlt* – *gpn* – *dbḥ* – *dbr* – *dqt* – *ḥlb* – *ḥmr* – *ḫlṣ* – *ḥmʾat* – *ḥmt* – *ḫpṯ* – *ḫrṯ* – *ṭbḫ* – *klb* – *klbt* – *llʾu* – *lsm* – *mgṯ* – *mdl* – *mrʾ* – *mrʾu* – *mtḥ* – *mṯpd* – *ngh* – *nhqt* – *nqbn* – *nqd* – *ssw* – *ˁgl* – *ˁglt* – *ˁr* – *ġbt* – *pḥl* – *pḥlt* – *pḥd* – *prt* – *ṣʾin* – *ṣmd* – *ql* – *rˁy* – *rġt* – *š* – *šgr* – *šḫp* – *šˁr* – *trbṣ* – *ṯʾat* – *ṯʾigt* – *ṯd* – *ṯr*

41. Fishing – hunting

ʾanhb – *ʾanḫr* – *dg* – *dgy* – *dgt* – *ḥẓ* – *yṣb* – *yry* – *kṯr* – *mrḥ* – *nd* – *nn* – *ntr* – *ġlp* *ym* – *ṣd* – *qn* – *qšt* – *rṯt* – *ṯkt*

42. Trade – transportation

ʾatnt – *bˁr* – *bšr* – *gpn* – *ḥmr* – *ḫrn* – *ybl* – *ydn* – *lʾk* – *mdl* – *mrkbt* – *mtḥ* – *mṯpd* – *nqbn* – *nšʾ* – *ssw* – *ˁms* – *ˁr* – *pḥl* – *pḥlt* – *ṣmd* – *rḥl* – *rkb* – *šlḥ* – *ṯkm*

43. Technology – tools

ʾulṯ – *bny* – *bˁl* – *gml* – *dm* – *hyn* – *ḥrš* – *ḫṭ* – *ḫs* – *ḫtr* – *yˁr* – *yṣq* – *yṣr* – *kbrt* – *kl* – *ksl* – *kp* – *kṯr* – *lbn* – *lṭš* – *lṯ* – *mznm* – *mṭ* – *mṭnt* – *mpḫm* – *mṣb* – *mṣbṭ* – *mṣrp* – *mrg* – *mšḫṭ* – *nb* – *sb* – *skn* – *skt* – *spsg* – *ˁdb* – *ˁsy* – *ˁšy* – *pʾat* – *pʾit* – *pḫr* – *plk* – *pslt* – *pršʾ* – *ṣmd* – *ṣmdm* – *qbt* – *qrˁ* – *qrṣ* – *qšt* – *rm* – *rq* – *šzr* – *šlḥ*

44. Materials – minerals (see also 13, 17, 18)

ʾabn – *ʾarz* – *ʾilqṣ* – *ʾiqnʾu* – *br* – *ḥtb* – *ḥpš* – *ḥmr* – *ḥrṣ* – *ḥṯṯ* – *ḫrṣ* – *ṯṯ* – *ẓẓ* – *yrq* – *ksp* – *mṯnt* – *spsg* – *ˁṣ* – *pḏ* – *pslt* – *rṯ* – *ṯlṯ*

45. Measuring

ʾamt – *ʾuṭ* – *ʾḫd* – *ʾrk* – *hn* – *ḥmšt* – *kbd* – *kmn* – *lg* – *md* – *mznm* – *mṣb* – *mšrr* – *ˁšrt* – *prs* – *rbˁt* – *rḥb* – *rm* – *šd* – *špl* – *ṯmq* – *ṯql*

46. Art – music

bdy – ḏmr – ṭb – yṣr – knr – lṭ – mn – mnt – mspr – mṣltm – nr – skn – sml – pḫr – qrṣ – šr – šrg – tp – ṯlb

47. Army – warriors

ʾib – ʾul – gmr – gpr – ḏmr – ḥyl – ḥl – mhr – nṯq – ʿdn – ʿqb – ʿrb – ġzr – pg – ṣbʾu – ṣrt – qrd – šnʾ – ṯnn

48. Weapons

ʾabn – ʾaymr – ʾarz – gd – dgl – ḥbš – ḥz – ḥrb – ḫt – ḫlpn – ygrš – kl – ksl – ktp – mṭ – mrḥ – mrkbt – mtn – npṣ – qn – qṣʿt – qšt

49. Safety – protection

ʾarbdd – brḥ – ḏmr – ḥl – ḥmyt – ḥtk – ḫpṭ – ḫpṭṭ – ydy – yqy – ytʿ – ytq – klʾ – lwy – mgdl – mṣd – mṣr – nd – ns – nġr – sgr – str – ʿḏr – ʿtd – plṭ – prṣ – ṣpr – šlm – šqd – tkn – ṯkm – ṯġr

50. Happiness

ʾanšt – ʾinš – ʾišryt – brlt – bšr – bšrt – gl – gmḏ – hdrt – ḥšn – ṭb – ṭbn – zḥq – ysm – ysmsmt – yp – kbd – kr – lyt – nʿm – nʿmy – npš – ʿlṣ – ġd – ply – prq – ṣhl – ṣḥq – rn – rqd – šmḫ – šmḫt – tsm – tp – tšyt

51. Love – marriage – childbirth

ʾagzr – ʾahbt – ʾaḫ – ʾaḫt – ʾalmnt – ʾalp – ʾaġzt – ʾarḫ – ʾarḫt – ʾatt – ʾitnn – ʾugr – ʾhb – bʾir – bdq – bny – bqʿ – brk – bšr – btl – btlt – bty – gzr – dd – ddy – hr – hry – hrt – zbl – zd – ḥbl – ḥbq – ḥdg – ḥmḥmt – ḥtl – ḫl – ḫlln – ḫtn – ẓš – ybm – ybmt – ybnt – yd – ydd – yḥd – yld – ylt – ymmt – ynq – ysmsmt – klt – ksʾan – ktr – ktrt – lwy – mdd – mhr – mḫr – mṣ – mr – mrġt – mt – mṯt – nd – nʿm – nšq – ʿl – ʿn – ʿp – ʿq – ʿry – ʿrs – ʿtk – ptḥ – qz – qny – qnṣ – qrṣ – rʾim – rḥm – rġt – rtq – škb – škllt – šm – šnʾ – šr – tbʿ – tnqt – tsm – tp – trḥ – ṯʾir – ṯʾr – ṯkḥ

52. Social relations – family

ʾab – ʾad – ʾadn – ʾahd – ʾaḫ – ʾaḫt – ʾalmnt – ʾamt – ʾanš – ʾaġzt – ʾary

– ʾaṯṯ – ʾulmn – ʾum – ʾumt – ʾgr – ʾnš – bḫṯ – bkr – bn – bnt – bt – gr
– dʿt – dr – hmlt – hry – zr – ḥbr – ḥzr – ḥtk – ḫpṯ – ḫr – ḫtn – ybm –
ybmt – yḥd – yld – yly – ymmt – yrṯ – ytm – ytmt – kdd – klt – lʾim – mʾinš
– mdd – mdʿ – mhr – mʿd – mrzḥ – mṯ – nkr – sd – ʿbd – ʿd – ʿdt – ʿdr
– ʿl – ʿm – ġrm – pḫr – ṣbrt – ṣġr – qbṣ – qny – rʿ – šb – šbḥ – šknt –
šm – špḥ – šrk – šrš – ṯʾir – ṯkl

53. Law – ethics – sin – pity

ʾaġzt – ʾidt – brt – bṯ – bṯt – gʾan – gʿr – gr – dn – zr – ḥnt – ḫṯʾ – ḫnp
– ẓn – yšr – kn – kny – lḥt – lšn – mṯpṭ – nʾṣ – nkr – nsy – nġš – ntb –
ʿllmy – ʿllmn – ġwy – ġz – ġlt – ġr – ġrm – pr – pšʿ – ṣdq – qdš – qlṣ
– qlt – rḥm – rḫnt – rk – rʿt – ršʿ – šrg – tbʿ – tdmm – ṯb – ṯkḫ – ṯpṭ – ṯpz – ṯš

54. Authority – power

ʾadn – ʾadr – ʾadt – ʾalʾiy – ʾalʾiyn – ʾan – ʾil – ʾul – ʾun – ʾgr – ʾdr
– ʾl – ʾmṣ – bʿl – bʿlt – bʿr – gbl – gmr – dn – drkt – zbl – ḥtk – ẓby – kḫṯ
– ksʾu – lʾan – lʾy – mlk – mlkt – mr – mšlt – mṯpṭ – mṯt – nmrt – srn
– ʿz – ʿṭrt – ʿẓm – ʿllmy – ʿllmn – ʿmq – ġyr – prln – prʿ – prʿt – qšr –
rbt – šlyṭ – šr – št – tkn – ṯʿ – ṯʿy – ṯpṭ

55. Possession – wealth

ʾiṣr – ʾḫd – ḫrṣ – yrq – yrṯ – ksp – lqḥ – nḥlt – ʿrẓ – ġz – ġrm – pḏ – pq
– qny – šns – ṯʾr

56. Subjection – obedience

ʾamt – ʾasr – ʾzr – ʾḫr – ʾsr – ʾṯr – gry – dll – hbr – ḥby – yṭq – kms –
krʿ – ktms – lʾy – lwy – lwn – mk – mr – nʿr – npl – nṣhy – ʿbd – ʿny
– ʿnn – ʿšr – ġyr – ġly – ġlm – ġlmt – ġr – prsḥ – ql – rky – rks – šby
– šbm – šḥy – šmʿ – špl – šqd – šqy – štm – ṯb

57. Courtesy – honouring – greeting

bḫṯ – bṯy – hbr – ḥn – yh – kbd – kny – krʿ – l – nʿm – nʿmt – npl – sʾd
– sʿd – ql – qm – rm – šḥy – šlm

58. Gifts – tribute – taxes

ʾargmn – *ʾitnn* – *ʾušn* – *ybl* – *yrṯ* – *ytn* – *ytnt* – *mgn* – *mhr* – *mzl* – *mnḥy* – *mᶜlt* – *mᶜrb* – *mġz* – *mtn* – *mtt* – *nzl* – *ᶜšrt* – *ġzy* – *pq* – *qdm* – *qrb* – *qry* – *qš* – *škr* – *šlḥ* – *šlm* – *tġzyt* – *trmmt* – *ṯkr*

59. Poverty – need

ʾabyn – *ʾalmnt* – *dl* – *ḥsr* – *ytm* – *ytmt* – *kly* – *ᶜny* – *ġmʾ* – *ġrm* – *ṣrk* – *rġb* – *škr* – *ṯkl*

60. Animosity – danger – war (see also 47, 48)

ʾabd – *ʾap* – *ʾib* – *ʾbd* – *ʾnš* – *ʾsr* – *bqᶜ* – *gd* – *ġḥṭ* – *gmr* – *gᶜr* – *gry* – *grš* – *dbr* – *dmy* – *dnt* – *drk* – *dṯ* – *hlm* – *hpk* – *hrg* – *wpṯ* – *ḥbṭ* – *ḥnp* – *ḥpy* – *ḥṣb* – *ḥrm* – *ḥš* – *ḥt* – *ḥtʾ* – *ṭbq* – *ṭᶜn* – *ṭrd* – *ydy* – *ymn* – *ypᶜ* – *yṣb* – *yry* – *kly* – *lwy* – *mdnt* – *mḥṣ* – *mḥr* – *mḥš* – *mlḥm* – *mlḥmt* – *mr* – *ngḥ* – *ngy* – *nd* – *ndp* – *nṭ* – *nky* – *ns* – *nsy* – *nsᶜ* – *npl* – *nṣḥy* – *ntr* – *nṯk* – *nṯq* – *sᶜy* – *ᶜdy* – *ᶜdn* – *ᶜllmy* – *ᶜllmn* – *ᶜlṣ* – *ᶜmd* – *ᶜmq* – *ᶜn* – *ᶜṣ* – *ᶜq* – *ᶜqb* – *ᶜrb* – *ᶜrp* – *ᶜšy* – *ᶜtk* – *prsḥ* – *ṣd* – *ṣm* – *ṣmt* – *ṣᶜṣ* – *ṣq* – *ṣr* – *ṣrt* – *ql* – *qlṣ* – *qry* – *qṯ* – *rdy* – *rġn* – *rš* – *šʾy* – *šby* – *šbm* – *šlm* – *šnʾ* – *šns* – *špl* – *šry* – *štm* – *tbᶜ* – *tlʾiyt* – *tšyt* – *ṯbr* – *ṯš*

61. Fear

ḥt – *ydᶜ* – *yrʾ* – *nd* – *ns* – *nġṣ* – *ġly* – *rġn* – *ṯbr* – *ṯm* – *ṯtᶜ*

62. Suffering – lament

ʾabyn – *ʾagzry* – *ʾi* – *ʾu* – *ʾudmᶜ* – *ʾun* – *ʾnḫ* – *ʾny* – *bd* – *bk* – *bky* – *bṯ* – *gl* – *dm* – *dmᶜ* – *dmᶜt* – *hdy* – *wpṯ* – *ḥkr* – *ḥmhm* – *ḥnp* – *ẓmʾ* – *y* – *ydy* – *yl* – *yrd* – *krb* – *lṣb* – *mzᶜ* – *mr* – *npl* – *nṣr* – *spd* – *ᶜgm* – *ᶜny* – *ġmʾ* – *pẓġ* – *ṣᶜq* – *ṣr* – *ṣt* – *šn* – *šrr* – *tnqt*

63. Disease – medicine

ʾabd – *ʾaḥdh* – *ʾakl* – *ʾapᶜ* – *ʾaškrr* – *ʾill* – *ʾbd* – *ʾkl* – *ʾml* – *ʾpq* – *dw* – *dwy* – *dlp* – *dm* – *dmrn* – *ḏmr* – *hm* – *zbl* – *zbln* – *ḥmṣ* – *ḥmt* – *ḥrḥrt* – *ḥrṣ* – *ḥtt* – *ḥsp* – *ḥrb* – *ḥrp* – *ḥš* – *ḥšt* – *ḥt* – *ṭmṯ* – *yblt* – *ydy* – *lṣb* –

mdw – *m^{c}m^c* – *mr* – *mrṣ* – *nḥy* – *nṭm* – *nqh* – *sm* – *^{c}dy* – *^{c}wr* – *^{c}lg* – *^{c}mt* – *^{c}qšr* – *^{c}rk* – *ġlt* – *pẓġ* – *prṭl* – *prsḥ* – *ṣml* – *ṣ^{c}ṣ* – *qzb* – *qrṣ* – *rp^ɔ* – *rp^{ɔ}u* – *šbt* – *šḫn* – *šmrr* – *šn* – *š^{c}tqt* – *tr^c* – *ṯb*

64. Death – burial – mourning

^{ɔ}akl – *^{ɔ}almnt* – *^{ɔ}i* – *^{ɔ}il^{ɔ}ib* – *^{ɔ}ill* – *^{ɔ}u* – *^{ɔ}udm^c* – *^{ɔ}ulmn* – *^{ɔ}un* – *^{ɔ}bd* – *^{ɔ}sp* – *bd* – *blmt* – *glḥ* – *gmn* – *dm* – *dm^c* – *dmrn* – *hdy* – *hmry* – *hrg* – *ḫlq* – *ḫpṯt* – *ḫrt* – *y* – *ybm* – *ybmt* – *ydy* – *ysmt* – *ytm* – *ytmt* – *m^{ɔ}izrtm* – *mdgt* – *mz^c* – *mk* – *mmt* – *mr* – *mt* – *mtt* – *n^{c}my* – *npl* – *skn* – *spd* – *^{c}mr* – *^{c}ry* – *pẓġ* – *pltt* – *ṣt* – *qbr* – *rḥm* – *š^{ɔ}y* – *šḫt* – *ṯkl*

65. Gods (see also 67, 68)

^{ɔ}abn – *^{ɔ}il* – *^{ɔ}il^{ɔ}ib* – *^{ɔ}ilh* – *^{ɔ}ilhm* – *b^{c}l* – *dgn* – *hd* – *hll* – *ḥrn* – *ḫrḫb* – *ẓẓ* – *yw* – *ym* – *yrḫ* – *kmṯ* – *kr* – *kṯr* – *ll* – *mlk* – *m^{c}d* – *mt* – *^{c}ttr* – *ġlm* – *pdr* – *pḥl* – *pḫr* – *ppšr* – *qdm* – *qdš* – *r^{ɔ}iṯ* – *ršp* – *šḥr* – *šlḥ* – *šmy* – *šnm* – *šr* – *šrk* – *ṯkmn*

66. Goddesses (see also 67, 68)

^{ɔ}arṣ – *^{ɔ}arṣy* – *^{ɔ}aṯrt* – *^{ɔ}ib* – *^{ɔ}ilht* – *^{ɔ}ilt* – *^{ɔ}išḫry* – *bq^{c}t* – *dmgy* – *dmqt* – *ḫprt* – *ṭly* – *ybrdmy* – *kṯrt* – *mlghy* – *mnt* – *nkl* – *^{c}nt* – *^{c}ttrt* – *pdry* – *pḥlt* – *ppšrt* – *prbḫt* – *qdš* – *rḥmy* – *špš* – *tlš* – *tq^{c}t* – *ṯlḥh* – *ṯtqt*

67. Divine epithets

^{ɔ}ab – *^{ɔ}ad* – *^{ɔ}adn* – *^{ɔ}aḫ* – *^{ɔ}aḫt* – *^{ɔ}al^{ɔ}iy* – *^{ɔ}al^{ɔ}iyn* – *^{ɔ}arḫ* – *^{ɔ}arḫt* – *^{ɔ}inš* – *bn* – *bny* – *b^{c}l* – *b^{c}lt* – *bt* – *btlt* – *gmr* – *d^{ɔ}it* – *d^{ɔ}u* – *dgy* – *hyn* – *zbl* – *ḥkm* – *ḥrš* – *ḥtk* – *ḥss* – *ḥtn* – *ybmt* – *ybnt* – *ydd* – *ymmt* – *kṯr* – *lb^{ɔ}u* – *ltpn* – *mdd* – *mhr* – *mlk* – *ngr* – *ngrt* – *nhr* – *nyr* – *n^{c}m* – *n^{c}mn* – *nrt* – *snnt* – *^{c}gl* – *^{c}ly* – *^{c}rẓ* – *ġlm* – *ġlmt* – *p^{ɔ}id* – *pr^{c}t* – *ṣqrn* – *qny* – *qnyt* – *qrd* – *rbt* – *rḥm* – *rḥmy* – *rkb* – *rp^{ɔ}u* – *šm* – *ṯd* – *ṯpṭ* – *ṯr*

68. Minor deities – demons – monsters – spirits

^{ɔ}akl – *^{ɔ}amrr* – *^{ɔ}aqht* – *^{ɔ}arṣ* – *^{ɔ}arš* – *^{ɔ}il^{ɔ}ib* – *^{ɔ}ilny* – *^{ɔ}ilš* – *^{ɔ}išt* – *^{ɔ}ugr* – *^{ɔ}ulkn* – *bkl* – *gpn* – *gtr* – *gtrm* – *dbb* – *ddn* – *ḏbb* – *hm* – *hrgb* – *ḥby* – *ḥrn* – *ḥrš* – *ḫnzr* – *ẓl* – *ẓn* – *ydy* – *yṭp* – *yṭpn* – *yqr* – *yṯq* – *kšd* – *kšp* – *ll* – *ltn*

– *mdb* – *mlʾak* – *mˁmˁ* – *nṭ* – *nqmd* – *nqp* – *sdn* – *ˁgml* – *ˁmṯtmr* – *ˁqq*
– *pḫr* – *prgl* – *ṣml* – *sˁṣ* – *qbʾ* – *qdmy* – *qṭr* – *qẓb* – *ql* – *qrʾ* – *rdmn* – *rdn*
– *rḥ* – *rpʾu* – *šd* – *šlyṭ* – *šˁtqt* – *tk* – *tnn* – *trmn* – *ṯr* – *ṯrmn*

69. Holy places

ʾaṯr – *ʾinbb* – *ʾuǵr* – *ʾur* – *bht* – *bmt* – *bt* – *gb* – *gg* – *ggt* – *dmrn* – *hkl*
– *hmry* – *ḥẓr* – *ḫršn* – *mhmrt* – *mˁbd* – *mṯb* – *mṯbt* – *ˁd* – *ṣpn* – *prq* – *qdš*
– *qˁl* – *šmm* – *trǵzz* – *ṯrmg*

70. Cultic functionaries

ʾadn – *bˁl* – *ḥl* – *khn* – *mḫll* – *mlk* – *mlkt* – *nˁm* – *nqd* – *ˁrb* – *ǵzr* – *rb*
– *šqy* – *šr* – *ṯˁy* – *ṯnn*

71. Revelation

ʾabn – *ʾg* – *ḏhrt* – *ḏrt* – *hdrt* – *ḥlm* – *lḫšt* – *ˁny* – *ˁṣ* – *prst* – *rgm* – *tʾant*

72. Cult – ritual (see also 64, 73)

ʾagn – *ʾilʾib* – *ʾurbt* – *ʾdm* – *br* – *brr* – *gmn* – *dk* – *dšn* – *ḏmr* – *hlk* – *ḥdṯ*
– *ḥl* – *ḥrm* – *ṯhr* – *yrḫ* – *lyt* – *mhy* – *mnt* – *mspr* – *mṣlt* – *mrzḥ* – *mrzˁ*
– *nsk* – *nšʾ* – *ntk* – *skn* – *ˁlm* – *ˁny* – *ˁrb* – *ˁrk* – *ˁrs* – *pslt* – *pˁnm* – *ṣbʾ*
– *ṣlm* – *qbʾ* – *qdš* – *qṭr* – *qrʾ* – *rʾiš* – *rgm* – *rḥṣ* – *rpʾu* – *šr* – *ṯˁy*

73. Sacrifice – offering

ʾagn – *ʾal* – *ʾalp* – *ʾannḫ* – *ʾap* – *ʾimr* – *ʾil* – *ʾuzr* – *ʾušpǵt* – *ʾuṯkl* – *bkr*
– *gd* – *gdlt* – *dbḥ* – *dd* – *dǵt* – *dǵtt* – *dqt* – *dṯt* – *zˁtr* – *zt* – *ztr* – *ḥtp* –
ḥṯ – *ḥmʾat* – *ḥmr* – *ḥrṣ* – *yḥmr* – *yn* – *ynt* – *yˁl* – *yṣq* – *yrd* – *kd* – *ksʾu*
– *ksm* – *ksp* – *ktn* – *kṯ* – *lbš* – *lḥm* – *llʾu* – *mgṯ* – *mdbḥ* – *mdbḥt* – *mhmrt*
– *mzn* – *mnt* – *mˁrb* – *mṣd* – *mṣlt* – *mrʾu* – *mšḫṯ* – *mtk* – *mtnt* – *nbt* –
nzl – *nsk* – *npl* – *npš* – *ntk* – *ˁly* – *ˁšr* – *ˁšrt* – *pgl* – *pḥd* – *qdm* – *qdš* –
qẓ – *ql* – *qlt* – *qmḥ* – *qmṣ* – *qṣ* – *qrb* – *qry* – *rmṣt* – *š* – *šdy* – *šḫṯ* – *šlm*
– *šmn* – *šnpt* – *šqy* – *šrp* – *šty* – *ṯǵzyt* – *tnr* – *trmmt* – *ṯd* – *ṯˁ* – *ṯˁy* – *ṯrm*

74. Vows

ʾalt – *ʾi* – *ʾidt* – *ʾdy* – *brt* – *gmr* – *mḏr* – *ndr* – *ǵrm* – *pr*

75. Magic

ʾun – ʾzr – ġḫṭ – ḥr – ḥrš – ydy – yṣq – kšp – lḫš – mn – mnt – ʿdy – qbʾ
– qšr – rky – rks

76. Prayer

ʾaḥl – ʾrš – by – bġy – ḥly – ydy – krʿ – ʿny – ġtr – ṣly – ṣlt – qbʾ – qrʾ
– šʾl – šmʿ

77. Blessing – cursing

ʾalt – ʾi – ʾimt – ʾr – brk – ḥn – ḥnt – ḫrm – lʾan – mr – nmrt – ṣm – ql